Filing Systems
and Records
Management

Gilbert Kahn, Ed.D.
Professor of Business Education
Montclair State College
Upper Montclair, New Jersey

Theodore Yerian, Ph.D.
Head of Departments of Business
Education and Secretarial Science
Oregon State University
Corvallis, Oregon

Jeffrey R. Stewart, Jr., Ed.D.
Professor of Business Education
Virginia Polytechnic Institute and State University
Blacksburg, Virginia

Filing Systems and Records Management

Second Edition

College Series

Gregg Division/McGraw-Hill Book Company
New York   St. Louis   Dallas   San Francisco
Düsseldorf   London   Mexico   Panama   Rio de Janeiro   Singapore
Sydney   Toronto

Filing Systems and Records Management, Second Edition
College Series

Copyright © 1971, 1962 by McGraw-Hill, Inc. All Rights Reserved. Printed in the United States of America. No part of this publication may be reproduced, stored in a retrieval system, or transmitted, in any form or by any means, electronic, mechanical, photocopying, recording, or otherwise, without the prior written permission of the publisher.
Library of Congress Catalog Card Number 72-88885

9 10 11 12 HDHD 798

ISBN 07-033231-2

Preface

The fallout of the information explosion has, without question, been paper work—more than the American businessman ever anticipated. For the college or business school graduate, a knowledge of the management of business records system is more important than ever as the volume and variety of paper work in the business office continue to expand. *Filing Systems and Records Management, Second Edition*—successor to *Progressive Filing and Records Management*—provides the basic principles and information that aim toward intelligent and efficient performance in managing and using records in the contemporary office.

The Instructional Program

The Textbook. The Second Edition, as the new title indicates, is oriented to a greater extent to a consideration of how records are managed within the context of a business system. While the popular features of the previous edition have been retained and updated, this edition also focuses upon paper flow within business systems, the three categories of records found in business systems, and flowcharts of systems as they relate to the management of business records.

Business forms and card records, which now undoubtedly exceed correspondence in volume, are given a great deal more emphasis and new treatment, both in the textbook and in the separate practice materials.

A great deal of added attention is given to automation and the newer methods of managing, storing, and retrieving records. New file equipment is described and generously illustrated.

The alphabetic indexing exercises, which formerly appeared in a chapter of the textbook as well as in the practice set, now appear in the Appendix and in the separate practice materials.

The Practice Materials. The separately published *Practice Materials for Filing Systems and Records Management, Second Edition*, is, of course, correlated with this textbook. These practice materials include job instructions, answer sheets, performance tests, file cards, cross-reference cards, miniature correspondence, cross-reference sheets, requisition forms, and a summary of the indexing rules. The 56 jobs in these materials provide practice in the following kinds of records systems: alphabetic card, alphabetic correspondence, numeric card (including serial or consecutive number, terminal digit, and middle digit), numeric correspondence, subject card, subject correspondence, geographic card, and geographic correspondence. Practice in

v

organizing systems, inspecting, indexing, coding, sorting, cross-referencing, charging out, replacing charged-out records, and retrieving records is provided.

The Tests. *Tests for Filing Systems and Records Management, Second Edition,* is a separate booklet providing nine objective tests. The Inventory Test may be used for placement purposes. Tests 1 through 7 are correlated with the twelve chapters of the textbook. Test 8 is a final examination, which covers the entire textbook.

The Instructor's Manual and Key. The *Instructor's Manual and Key* contains teaching suggestions, time schedules, and complete keys to the textbook, practice materials, and test exercises.

Supporting Materials

Gregg Filing Wall Charts. This set of eight *Gregg Filing Wall Charts,* in two colors, summarizes and illustrates the following filing and records management procedures and activities: Steps Before Filing; Alphabetic Filing; Alphabetic Guide and Folder Arrangement; Numeric Filing; Geographic Filing; Subject Filing; Finding Lost Records; and Records Retention, Transfer, and Disposal. These charts are designed for either permanent or temporary display in the classroom, depending upon whether the instructor wishes to use them solely for teaching purposes or for both teaching and continuous reference and reinforcement purposes.

Gregg Filing Transparencies. Each of the 20 indexing rules in the Gregg filing and records management textbooks is presented on a two-color transparency. The accompanying specially designed slider masks permit the instructor to teach the application of the rules step by step. The 20 transparencies, together with correlated guide notes for the instructor, are bound in a Flipatran binder.

Filmstrips. The set of *Progressive Filing* filmstrips consists of four 35-mm filmstrips, with sound and in color. These filmstrips and the accompanying records, which are recorded at $33\frac{1}{3}$ rpm, provide instruction in the 20 indexing rules presented in Gregg filing and records management textbooks and, in addition, describe efficient filing procedures.

Workbook Exercises. *Workbook Exercises in Alphabetic Filing, Second Edition,* is a 48-page workbook giving the student additional practice in alphabetic card filing. Each of the 20 indexing rules is presented and illustrated, followed by "cards" that are to be removed and filed in the proper order. In addition to the drills on the rules, there are five review exercises embodying all the rules of alphabetic filing. In all, there are 720 names on cards for practice purposes.

Gilbert Kahn
Theodore Yerian
Jeffrey R. Stewart, Jr.

Contents

Contents

1 Records Management and Business Systems

How does the complex structure known as the American free enterprise system of business operate so smoothly? What is it that enables countless consumer demands to be translated into billions of dollars' worth of products and services? Intense competition, creative salesmanship, and clever innovation are often cited as the principal answers. But a large part of the answer lies in the fact that the businessman has made more effective use of *business records* than has been done ever before in history. Business records are the movers of the facts and figures that every businessman needs in order to operate. Without systems that put the right record into the hands of the right person at the right time, any business would cease to operate.

Office Systems

Every business record—a form, a letter, a contract, an invoice, or an order —exists as part of an administrative operation of the business. For example, an order is part of a purchasing system; a time-card is part of a payroll system. Administrative systems often operate separately from one another, especially in medium to large firms. Thus, you might find that a business has a sales department, a purchasing department, a payroll department, and an inventory control department. Each of these departments receives, creates, processes, and transmits papers and records that facilitate the work. Business records, then, are vital to the day-to-day operations of any enterprise. A study of

1

the management of business records and the systems of which they are a part is an important part of the background needed for entrance into business occupations.

Records Management and Filing

At one time, the management of records was considered to mean the storage, retrieval, and protection of business papers—basically, filing. Today, of course, records management includes not only filing but also the creation, control, use, and disposition of records. Records management and filing are not the kinds of responsibilities that are usually assigned to one person or department in a business. Everyone who handles business records needs to be knowledgeable in the subject of filing and records management and to be aware of the importance of correct creation, storage, protection, control, use, and disposition of records. Although some large companies have specialists who deal with paperwork problems, such specialists cannot possibly oversee all the paperwork activities of the typical firm.

Dependence of Office System on Records

To see how vitally dependent on records an office system is, let us trace the records that might be used to support a typical credit sales system.

The system illustrated shows a credit sales system in a department store. The flowchart shows the steps that are taken from the time the customer applies for credit until he receives his first monthly bill. Following are the steps as they are numbered in the illustration:

1. The customer decides to open a charge account; he fills out an application form.
2. The application form is sent to the credit office, where the customer's credit is found to be satisfactory.
3. The credit office mails a charge plate to the customer.
4. The credit office files the customer's application for credit.
5. The customer, using his charge plate, buys merchandise.
6. The salesclerk writes a sales slip in duplicate; he gives the original to the customer and keeps the carbon copy.
7. The sales slip copy is sent to an accounts receivable clerk, who posts it to the customer's account.
8. The sales slip copy is microfilmed.
9. The customer's account is filed, awaiting additional daily postings of sales.
10. Monthly, the customer's account is retrieved from the file and delivered to a photocopy machine operator.

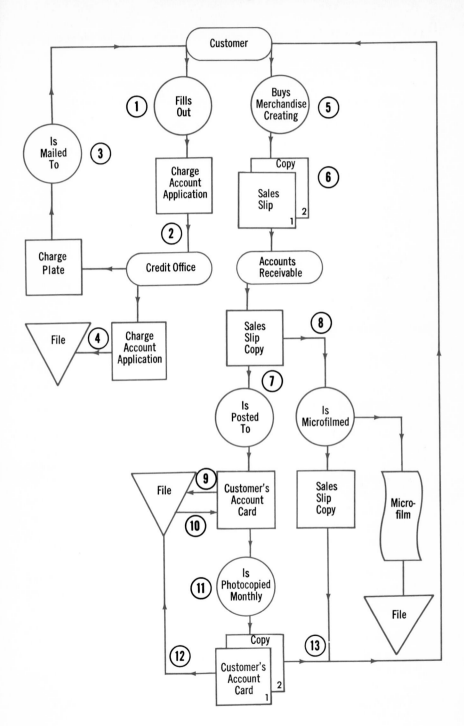

11. A copy of the customer's account is prepared on the photocopy machine.
12. The original copy of the customer's account is refiled.
13. The photocopy of the customer's account is mailed to the customer as his monthly bill with the carbon copies of the saleschecks.

It is easy to see from the flowchart that the records themselves are important, as are the ways in which they are used and managed. The importance of any one record can be seen by imagining that it has been eliminated from the system. Suppose, for example, that the sales slip were eliminated. Then there would be no source document to post to the customer's account, the customer would never receive a receipt or a bill, and the store might never receive payment from the customer. Therefore, the sales slip is an essential link in the sales system illustrated.

The importance of the management of the records can also be shown by imagining that incorrect or incomplete information has been recorded on the records, or that records have been lost or filed in the wrong place. For example, suppose that a completed sales slip copy is misplaced before it is delivered to the accounts receivable clerk. The recording of the sale will be omitted unless a procedure is established to control all sales slips. Such a procedure might be to prenumber all sales slips so that accounts receivable can keep a running check to see that every number is accounted for.

Life Cycle of a Business Record

From the foregoing example, you can see that the overall management of records is basic to the operation of business. The knowledgeable businessman is not only concerned with how his records fit into his business systems; he is also aware of the complete life cycle of each record that is used in his firm and knows that some provision must be made for the eventual transfer and disposition of records.

The life cycle of a business record involves five stages: (1) creation or receipt, (2) storage and protection, (3) use, (4) transfer, and (5) disposal.

Creation or Receipt. The number of records handled daily within a typical organization is staggering. A large retail store, for example, will create hundreds of records every day—letters, advertising copy, accounting statements, purchase orders, sales slips, checks, receiving tickets, and so on. Also, the same store receives hundreds, perhaps thousands, of pieces of correspondence daily—applications for credit, invoices, order letters, credit reports, price lists, catalogs, and so on. Hundreds of man-hours are spent daily in handling these records. Without the records the business simply could not operate. Most records eventually find their way into one type of file or another so that they may be referred to when needed as a basis for important managerial decisions and action.

Storage and Protection. When the decision is made to retain business papers, provision must be made for storing and protecting them during their useful lifetime. Because of their unusual size or shape, records such as large blue-prints in an architect's office require equipment especially made for storing them. Extremely important records, such as legal papers, are stored in insulated cabinets capable of withstanding extreme heat in case of fire. Any record worth retaining should be properly housed so that it can be located rapidly when needed and so that it is always adequately protected.

Use. Records are stored for one principal reason: use. Only records that will be needed for later reference are worth the time required to store them. Office space and filing equipment are too expensive to be used to "hide" papers that no one will ever use. Knowing which records will—and which will not —be used again requires knowledge about the business and a fair amount of judgment.

Transfer. As records become inactive—referred to only infrequently—they should be culled from the files to make room for active records. Besides occupying valuable office space and equipment, inactive records get in the way of the efficient use of active ones. Periodically, then, infrequently used records should be removed from the main files and placed in *transfer files*. Transfer files look somewhat like regular files, except that the containers are less expensive (usually pressboard containers), and they are kept in less accessible locations, such as the basement, where floor space is less expensive than in the main office.

Disposal. The last stage in the records management cycle is the disposal of records. Of course, all records that no longer serve a useful purpose should be destroyed. The decision as to when records are to be destroyed is usually made by management. The policy is determined by legal considerations and by the special needs of the business. At any rate, some definite plan should be set up by management for the periodic destruction of records that are no longer of value to the organization.

The Importance of Filing

Filing is that part of records management which deals largely with the classification, arrangement, and storage of business records so that they may be quickly located when needed. Nearly every entry-level job in an office requires a knowledge of filing.

Organizations have been known to fail because they did not recognize the importance of well-organized records. On the other hand, many enterprises have attributed much of their success to the fact that important business decisions could be made easily and quickly because the necessary information was immediately available.

Visualize a busy executive who is talking on the telephone and who suddenly needs information about a contract bid that was mailed a few days earlier. He recalls that the bid was approximately a quarter of a million dollars, but his copy of the letter has been filed. He tells his secretary to find the letter containing the quotation while he continues the telephone conversation. What might happen if that letter cannot be found—at least in time to be of use during the telephone conversation? "For want of a letter the contract was lost" could be a modern counterpart to the old saying, "For want of a nail the shoe was lost."

Organizations of every type—business and professional, large and small—need to store records for future reference. All these records—important facts about products, statistical data, information about employees and customers, facts about suppliers, and a myriad of other data—should be quickly available through systematic filing procedures. Thus, all records should be stored for safety as well as accessibility.

The importance of systematic filing is also demonstrated by a study showing that 43 percent of the businesses whose records were destroyed by fire or other causes were not able to resume operations! The storing of records so that they are protected from loss is a vital part of the filing process. In some cases, records may need special protection against fire; in others, against weather conditions. In all cases, however, all records worth keeping should be protected against the risk of being misplaced. Misfiled records can cost a firm many hundreds or thousands of dollars. Opportunities to take advantage of discounts on bills may be lost if the invoices cannot be located; big sales cannot be closed when the necessary specifications, documents, or contracts are not readily available. The time alone that is lost by looking for improperly stored records may be worth many hundreds of dollars.

Filing activities and equipment are expensive. To help keep filing costs to a minimum, good judgment must be exercised in choosing the records to be kept. Not everything should be filed—only those records that are essential to the efficient operation of the organization. The materials that are to be stored in the files come from two sources: (1) those that originate outside the organization, such as incoming letters, reports, contracts, catalogs, statements, and invoices; and (2) those that originate within the organization, such as copies of outgoing letters, reports, contracts, and invoices. Materials from outside the organization will usually be original copies; those from within the organization will usually be carbon copies or photocopies of originals.

Office Employment and Filing

Because records are so important in any organization, they influence, in some way, the activities of every employee. Those who work in the office are especially concerned with records—creating them and later finding and using them.

A secretary without a working knowledge of filing and filing systems is greatly handicapped. Often she is responsible for keeping her employer's personal files. In a small organization she may be requested to set up a filing system for the organization or to reorganize an existing system.

"Miss Murphy, please get me a copy of the letter we wrote to the Centerville Brick Company about the building materials for the new lab," is a common type of request made of a secretary. Not only is she expected to know how to find the letter, but she is also expected to find it quickly. No secretary should consider her training complete without a thorough knowledge of filing procedures, techniques, and records management.

For many office workers, filing is a full-time activity. As organizations grow, their filing functions become more involved and demanding. Files are often kept in central locations, especially in larger organizations, because the centralization eliminates the need for duplication of records in separate department files. From these central locations, records can be more easily obtained by all departments that may need them for reference purposes. The specialized file worker has become an important person in the operation of the office. File supervisors, of course, are needed to oversee the file workers. Opportunities for advancement are excellent for those who have supervisory ability and wish to assume responsibilities.

Most office workers make use of office records in some capacity daily. Typists, accountants, stenographers, key-punch operators, computer operators, and general clerical workers all use files frequently. No office worker's job preparation is complete without a knowledge of filing. Although he may not be directly involved in the filing process, his effectiveness will be increased if he knows the problems of the file worker and understands the importance of systematic filing.

A thorough knowledge of filing is essential for the efficient supervision and management of an office. The office manager should be so well informed about filing techniques and records administration that he is able to determine such matters as the type of filing system to be used, the equipment to be purchased, and the personnel needed to maintain the files.

Basic Filing Concepts

Even before you started this formal study of filing, you had become familiar with some of the basic concepts of filing. Every time you looked for a name and number in the telephone directory, you were selecting information from a book organized around filing principles. The names are arranged alphabetically, and your knowledge of the alphabet helped you to find the name you wanted. The telephone directory is an example of one of the two basic methods of arranging records for easy location—by *name*. The other method is by *number*. An example is a filing system in an insurance company's home office, where records are requested by policy number.

A *caption* is a name or a number used to identify records for filing purposes. For example, if it is decided that a letter should be kept in the *Bass and Trent Company* file, the company name is the caption.

In *alphabetic* systems the captions are names of people and organizations; in *geographic* systems, the names of places. In *subject* systems the captions are names of objects or categories; while in *numeric* systems the captions are numbers.

In summary, then, it can be said that records are kept in files under *names* or *numbers*. The alphabet, however, is the basis for *most* filing systems, even those in which records are stored by number.

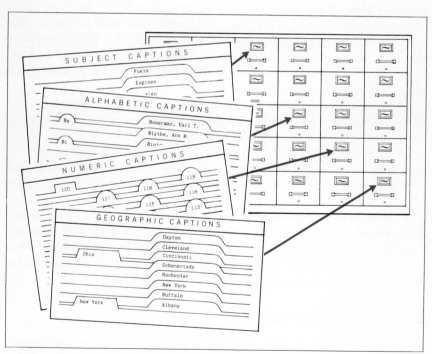

The four basic file captions can often be found in the files of a single office.

Questions and Problems

1. Name several departments that a business might have to facilitate the various functions of the business.
2. What activities are included in a broad definition of records management?
3. What are some of the records that are kept for a typical sales system in a department store?
4. Why is each record named in the answer to Question 3 basic to the operation of the sales system?
5. What are the five stages in the life cycle of a business record?
6. What are the primary activities associated with filing?
7. From what two sources does material to be filed originate?
8. Name several office occupations in which a knowledge of filing is especially important.
9. What are the two basic methods of arranging records?
10. Define the term *caption*.
11. Name four types of captions that might be found in the files of a business office.

Case Problems in Records Management

1. John Williams owns a service station. He told a friend of his, Ted Martin, that he does not need to keep an organized set of records. Ted said that John should keep well-planned files. With whom do you agree? Why?
2. Irene Jorgensen, who is employed as a file worker in a large insurance company, told a co-worker that the keeping of records is more important in a large organization than it is in a small one. Her co-worker disagrees. Who is right? Why?
3. Upon graduation from college, Frieda Webber expects to work in her uncle's large real estate office. She says that she does not plan to take a course in records management because it will not be useful in her job. Do you agree or disagree with her? Why?

Alphabetic Indexing

As YOU LEARNED in Chapter 1, records are identified by their captions, which may be either words or numbers. This chapter presents the rules for determining correct captions for alphabetic systems of records management. The act of determining the caption by which a record is identified and of determining the proper order of words or numbers in that caption is known as *indexing*. For example, you alphabetically index the name *Glenn Krieger* when you decide that in order to find his name in the telephone directory, you will have to look under *K* and not *G*. Obviously, standard rules have to be observed by everyone in selecting and arranging captions. If each person who does filing were to make up his own rules, the results would be chaotic: only the person who did the actual filing would be able to find the records—if indeed even he could.

Alphabetic Indexing Rules

The alphabetic indexing rules on the following pages make use of two terms with which you should be familiar: *alphabetizing* and *unit*.

Alphabetizing is the arranging of names according to the alphabetic sequence of their letters. For example, the names *Lewis, Perkins,* and *Vance* are arranged in correct alphabetic sequence, since in the alphabet *L* precedes *P* and *P* precedes *V*. The names *Parks, Perkins,* and *Prichard* are also arranged in correct alphabetic sequence; although the first letter in each name is the same, the second letter, which is different in each name, is in correct alphabetic sequence—the *a* in *Parks* precedes the *e* in *Perkins,* and the *e* in *Perkins* precedes the *r* in *Prichard.* The names *Rodgers, Roebuck,* and *Rollins* are arranged in correct alphabetic sequence; although the first two letters in each name are the same, the third letter, which is different in each name, is arranged in correct alphabetic sequence.

Each part of the name of a person or an organization used in indexing is a *unit.* The name *Richard T. Simpson* contains three units: (1) *Richard,* (2) *T.* and (3) *Simpson.* The company name *Willamette Valley Packing Company* contains four units; *Johnson City Shoe Company, Inc.,* five units.

Twenty rules for alphabetic indexing are presented in this chapter. After each four rules, you should refer to the *Practice Materials for Filing Systems and Records Management* and complete the jobs specified. (If the practice set is not available, refer to the Appendix of this book for practice exercises.)

Rule 1. Individual Names

Transpose and alphabetize the names of individuals in this order: surname, or last name, first; given name, or first name, second; and middle name, if any, third.

NAME	PROPER INDEXING ORDER
Thomas Andrew Glover	Glover, Thomas Andrew
Rhoda Phillips	Phillips, Rhoda
Evelyn Rowe	Rowe, Evelyn

Rule 2. Alphabetic Order

Names are alphabetized by comparing the first unit in each name, letter by letter. The second units are considered only when the first units are identical. The third units are considered only when both the first and second are identical, and so on.

	INDEXING UNITS		
	UNIT 1	UNIT 2	UNIT 3
Robert James Anderson	Anderson	Robert	James
Florence M. Apperson	Apperson	Florence	M.
Patricia L. Apperson	Apperson	Patricia	L.
Stanley Richard Collins	Collins	Stanley	Richard
Stanley Robert Collins	Collins	Stanley	Robert

Rule 3. Surname Alone or With Initials

A surname, when used alone, precedes the same surname with a first name or initial. A surname with only a first initial precedes the same surname with a complete first name beginning with the same letter as the initial. This rule is sometimes stated, "Nothing comes before something."

	INDEXING UNITS		
	UNIT 1	UNIT 2	UNIT 3
Davenport	Davenport		
J. Davenport	Davenport	J.	
John Davenport	Davenport	John	
John H. Davenport	Davenport	John	H.
John Henry Davenport	Davenport	John	Henry

Rule 4. Surname Prefixes

A surname prefix is *not* a separate indexing unit, but it is considered part of the surname. These prefixes include: *d', D', Da, de, De, Del, Des, Di, Du, Fitz, La, Le, M', Mac, Mc, O', St., Van, Van der, Von, Von der,* and others. The prefixes *M', Mac,* and *Mc* are indexed exactly as they are spelled. The prefix *St.* is indexed as though spelled out—*Saint*.

	INDEXING UNITS		
	UNIT 1	UNIT 2	UNIT 3
Daniel De Lancey	De Lancey	Daniel	
James T. LaFever	LaFever	James	T.
Robert L. MacDeeney	MacDeeney	Robert	L.
Robert L. McDeeney	McDeeney	Robert	L.
Homer W. St. Clair	Saint Clair	Homer	W.
Helen Van der Veer	Van der Veer	Helen	

Captions on Cards

Several recommendations are given here for typing information on file cards.

1. Type the units of a name in the order in which they are considered for indexing. This is referred to as proper indexing order.
2. Leave a two-space left margin, and begin typing on the second line from the top.
3. Words may be typed in all capital letters, or only the first letter of each word need be capitalized. Choose one style and be consistent in using that style.

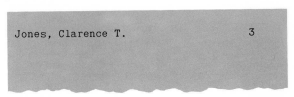

```
Jones, Clarence T.                          3
```

A Name Typed in Correct Position on a File Card

4. For abbreviations and symbols, follow the style used by the person or company whose name you are typing. For example, in the name *Jones, Perkins & Jones, Inc.*, type the *&* sign and the abbreviation *Inc.* It is common practice to use abbreviated firm name endings, such as *Co.* and *Inc.*, with all organization names in order to conserve space on the cards.
5. Punctuation is also a matter of company preference. Consistency is the key word, of course. Here are some examples:

Jones, Clarence T.	Standard Punctuation (Used by Most People)
Jones Clarence T	No Punctuation
Jones Clarence T	Extra Space——No Punctuation
Jones/Clarence/T	Oblique Line Separators

Names Involving Indexing Rules 1, 2, 3, and 4 As They Should Be Typed on File Cards and Sequenced

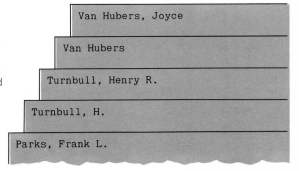

```
                    Van Hubers, Joyce

                Van Hubers

            Turnbull, Henry R.

        Turnbull, H.

    Parks, Frank L.
```

Filing Practice

Complete Jobs 1 and 2 in the practice set, or refer to the Appendix for practice exercises.

Rule 5. Firm Names

The units in firm and institution names are considered in the same sequence as written when they do not contain the *complete* name of an individual.   When a foreign word is the initial word, it is *not* a separate indexing unit but is considered part of the word that follows.

	INDEXING UNITS		
	UNIT 1	UNIT 2	UNIT 3
Gallagher Trucking Service	Gallagher	Trucking	Service
Les Parfums Importers	Les Parfums	Importers	
Murphy Cleaners	Murphy	Cleaners	
Murphy Grocery Company	Murphy	Grocery	Company
Oregon Fabric Company	Oregon	Fabric	Company
Oregon Fabric Products	Oregon	Fabric	Products

Rule 6. Firm Names Containing Complete Individual Names

When the firm or institution name includes the complete name of an individual, the units in the individual's name are transposed.   Any one of the following combinations constitutes a complete name: (a) first initial and surname; (b) first and middle initials and surname; (c) given name and surname; (d) given name, middle initial or name, and surname.

	INDEXING UNITS			
	UNIT 1	UNIT 2	UNIT 3	UNIT 4
Harold T. Benson Realtors	Benson	Harold	T.	Realtors
Benson Machine Works	Benson	Machine	Works	
Caldwell Hardware Center	Caldwell	Hardware	Center	
C. John Daley, Jewelers	Daley	C.	John	Jewelers
F. Daley, Builders	Daley	F.	Builders	

Rule 7. Article "The"

"The" is *not* a unit and is disregarded in indexing.   (When writing names on filing cards and folders, if "the" occurs at the beginning of a name, it is placed at the end in parentheses.   If "the" occurs in the middle of a name, it is placed in parentheses but is not moved.)

INDEXING UNITS			
UNIT 1	UNIT 2	UNIT 3	UNIT 4

	UNIT 1	UNIT 2	UNIT 3	UNIT 4
Barton the Plumber	Barton	Plumber		
The Blue Sea Dairy	Blue	Sea	Dairy	
The Henry J. Brandt Nursery	Brandt	Henry	J.	Nursery
The Brandt Nursery Farm	Brandt	Nursery	Farm	
Jack the Fisherman Lodge	Jack	Fisherman	Lodge	

Rule 8. Hyphenated Names

Hyphenated words in a firm name are indexed as *separate* units. Hyphenated surnames of individuals are considered as *one* indexing unit; this applies also to hyphenated names of individuals whose complete names are part of a firm name.

	INDEXING UNITS			
	UNIT 1	UNIT 2	UNIT 3	UNIT 4
Brick-Sea Builders	Brick-	Sea	Builders	
Linder-Jones Automotive Works	Linder-	Jones	Automotive	Works
Jane P. Linder-Jones	Linder-Jones	Jane	P.	
Joseph Linder-Jones Company	Linder-Jones	Joseph	Company	

Names Involving Indexing Rules 5, 6, 7, and 8 As They Should Be Typed on File Cards and Sequenced

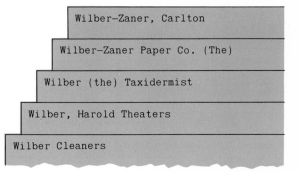

Wilber–Zaner, Carlton

Wilber–Zaner Paper Co. (The)

Wilber (the) Taxidermist

Wilber, Harold Theaters

Wilber Cleaners

Filing Practice

Complete Jobs 3 and 4 in the practice set, or refer to the Appendix for practice exercises.

Rule 9. Abbreviations

Abbreviations are indexed as though the words represented were written
in full.   Single letters other than abbreviations are considered as separate
indexing units.

	INDEXING UNITS			
	UNIT 1	UNIT 2	UNIT 3	UNIT 4
AZA Club	A	Z	A	Club
Chas. Bradford Chemical Co.	Bradford	Charles	Chemical	Company
Columbia Gorge Dist.	Columbia	Gorge	District	
Drexel St. Corp.	Drexel	Street	Corporation	
Gen. Audit Co.	General	Audit	Company	

Rule 10. Conjunctions, Prepositions, and Firm Endings

Conjunctions and prepositions, such as *and, &, for, in, of,* are *not* units
and are disregarded in indexing.   On filing cards and folders, these words
are written in their normal sequence.   Firm endings, such as *Bros., Co.,
Corp., Inc., Ltd., Mfg.,* and *Son,* are indexing units.

	INDEXING UNITS			
	UNIT 1	UNIT 2	UNIT 3	UNIT 4
B and T School	B	T	School	
Burns & Son	Burns	Son		
Full-of-Fun Park Corp.	Full-	Fun	Park	Corporation
Higgens and Son, Ltd.	Higgens	Son	Limited	
Luther Jones and Associates	Jones	Luther	Associates	

Rule 11. One or Two Words

Names that may be written as either one or two words are indexed as
one unit.

	INDEXING UNITS			
	UNIT 1	UNIT 2	UNIT 3	UNIT 4
Inter State Carrier Corp.	Inter State	Carrier	Corporation	
The Interstate Development Agency	Interstate	Develop-ment	Agency	
North West Bus Co.	North West	Bus	Company	
Northwest Travel Bureau, Inc.	Northwest	Travel	Bureau	Incorpo-rated

Rule 12. Compound Geographic Names

The parts of compound geographic names are separate indexing units, except when the first part of the name is not an English word, such as the *Los* in *Los Angeles*.

	INDEXING UNITS			
	UNIT 1	UNIT 2	UNIT 3	UNIT 4
Las Vegas Valley Cleaners	Las Vegas	Valley	Cleaners	
Los Alamos Candy Importers	Los Alamos	Candy	Importers	
New Rochelle Land Co.	New	Rochelle	Land	Company
New York Bakeries, Inc.	New	York	Bakeries	Incorporated

Names Involving Index-ing Rules 9, 10, 11, and 12 As They Should Be Typed on File Cards and Sequenced

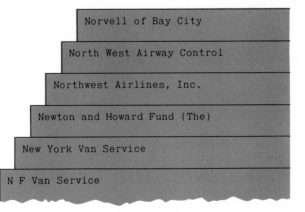

Norvell of Bay City

North West Airway Control

Northwest Airlines, Inc.

Newton and Howard Fund (The)

New York Van Service

N F Van Service

Filing Practice

Complete Jobs 5 and 6 in the practice set or refer to the Appendix for practice exercises.

Rule 13. Titles and Degrees

Titles and degrees are *not* units and are disregarded in indexing.   Terms that designate seniority, such as *Jr., Sr., 2d,* are indexing units.   On filing cards and folders, titles, degrees, and seniority terms are enclosed in parentheses and placed at the end of the name.

Exception A: When the name of an individual consists of a title and one name only, such as *Queen Elizabeth,* the name is *not* transposed and the title *is* an indexing unit.

Exception B: When a title is the initial word of a firm or association name, it *is* an indexing unit.

	INDEXING UNITS		
	UNIT 1	UNIT 2	UNIT 3
General Houser	General	Houser	
Dr. John Miller, Jr.	Miller	John	Junior
John Miller, Sr.	Miller	John	Senior
Queen Anne Decorators	Queen	Anne	Decorators

Rule 14. Possessives

When a word ends with *apostrophe s,* the *s* is disregarded in indexing. However, when a word ends in *s apostrophe,* because the *s* is part of the original word, it *is* considered.   This rule is sometimes stated, "Consider everything up to the apostrophe."

	INDEXING UNITS		
	UNIT 1	UNIT 2	UNIT 3
Backman's Motor Court	Backman	Motor	Court
The Backman News Agency	Backman	News	Agency
Byers the Auctioneer	Byers	Auctioneer	
Byers' Rug Cleaners	Byers'	Rug	Cleaners
John P. Byerson	Byerson	John	P.

Rule 15. U. S. and Foreign Government Names

Names pertaining to the federal government are indexed under *United States Government* and subdivided, first by title of the department, and then by bureau, division, commission, or board.

Names pertaining to foreign governments are indexed under names of countries and subdivided, first by title of the department, and then by bureau, division, commission, or board.

Phrases such as *Department of, Bureau of, Division of, Commission of, Board of,* when used in titles of governmental bodies, are disregarded in indexing. On filing cards and folders, these phrases in governmental titles are enclosed in parentheses and placed after the words they modify. Such phrases, however, *are* indexing units in nongovernmental names.

	INDEXING UNITS			
	UNIT 1	UNIT 2	UNIT 3	UNIT 4
Dominion of Canada Department of Finance	Canada	Finance		
Citizens Education Committee for Schools	Citizens	Education	Committee	Schools
Union of South Africa Dept. of Education	South	Africa	Education	
U. S. Dept. of Defense	United	States	Government	Defense
United States Steel Co.	United	States	Steel	Company
West Indies Fisheries	West	Indies	Fisheries	

Rule 16. Other Political Divisions

Names pertaining to other political divisions are indexed under the name of the political division followed by its classification, such as *state, county,* or *city,* and then subdivided by the title of the department, bureau, division, commission, or board.

	INDEXING UNITS			
	UNIT 1	UNIT 2	UNIT 3	UNIT 4
Benton County Reclamation Bureau	Benton	County	Reclamation	
City Water Department Corvallis, Oregon	Corvallis	City	Water	
Michigan State, Committee on Lakes and Rivers	Michigan	State	Lakes	Rivers
Department of Highways, State of Pennsylvania	Pennsylvania	State	Highways	

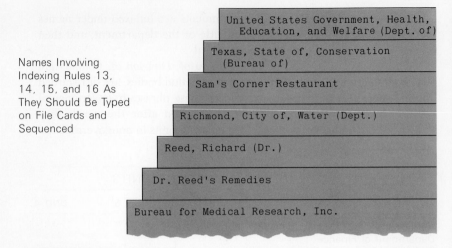

Names Involving
Indexing Rules 13,
14, 15, and 16 As
They Should Be Typed
on File Cards and
Sequenced

```
United States Government, Health,
  Education, and Welfare (Dept. of)

Texas, State of, Conservation
  (Bureau of)

Sam's Corner Restaurant

Richmond, City of, Water (Dept.)

Reed, Richard (Dr.)

Dr. Reed's Remedies

Bureau for Medical Research, Inc.
```

Filing Practice

Complete Jobs 7 and 8 in the practice set or refer to the Appendix for practice exercises.

Rule 17. Numbers

A number in a name is considered as though written in words and is indexed as *one* unit. Numbers over 1,000, such as 1,205, should be indexed *twelve hundred five* and not as *one thousand two hundred five*.

	INDEXING UNITS			
	UNIT 1	UNIT 2	UNIT 3	UNIT 4
Carlos of 31 Plaza Road	Carlos	Thirty-one	Plaza	Road
Century at 71st Mall	Century	Seventy-first	Mall	
1900 Rose Manor	Nineteen hundred	Rose	Manor	
60th & Belmont Precinct	Sixtieth	Belmont	Precinct	
29th Street Grocery & Restaurant	Twenty-ninth	Street	Grocery	Restaurant

Rule 18. Addresses

When the same name appears with different addresses, it should be alphabetized according to city or town. The state is considered only when there is duplication of both individual or company name and city name. If the same name is located at different addresses within the same city, then it should be alphabetized by streets. If the same name is located at more than one address on the same street, then it should be arranged from the lowest to the highest house or building number.

	INDEXING UNITS				
	UNIT 1	UNIT 2	UNIT 3	UNIT 4	UNIT 5
Doss Studios 231 Ankeny Street, Portland	Doss	Studios	Portland	Ankeny	Street 231
Doss Studios 592 Ankeny Street, Portland	Doss	Studios	Portland	Ankeny	Street 592
Doss Studios Williams Street, Seattle	Doss	Studios	Seattle	Williams	Street
Dowler Brokerage Ashland, Texas	Dowler	Brokerage	Ashland	Texas	
Dowler Brokerage Peoria, Illinois	Dowler	Brokerage	Peoria	Illinois	

Rule 19. Bank Names

Bank names are indexed first by city, then by bank name, with the state considered only if there is duplication of city and bank names. On filing cards and folders, the state is enclosed in parentheses and placed last.

	INDEXING UNITS				
	UNIT 1	UNIT 2	UNIT 3	UNIT 4	UNIT 5
Prothro Savings Bank, Helena, Mont.	Helena	Prothro	Savings	Bank	
Citizens Export Bank, Lamar, Mo.	Lamar	Citizens	Export	Bank	
First National Bank Longton, N. M.	Longton	First	National	Bank	
New Jersey State Bank, Morris, N. J.	Morris	New	Jersey	State	Bank
First Nat. Bank Newark, Del.	Newark	First	National	Bank	Delaware
First Nat. Bank Newark, N. J.	Newark	First	National	Bank	New Jersey

Rule 20. Married Women

The legal name of a married woman is the one used for indexing. Legally, the surname is the only part of her husband's name a woman assumes when she marries. Her legal name, therefore, could be either (1) her own first and middle names together with her husband's surname or (2) her own first name and maiden surname together with her husband's surname. On file cards and folders, *Mrs.* is placed in parentheses at the end of the name; the husband's first and middle names or initials are enclosed in parentheses and placed below the woman's legal name.

	INDEXING UNITS		
	UNIT 1	UNIT 2	UNIT 3
Mrs. Harold Bates (Marjorie Roslyn)	Bates	Marjorie	Roslyn
Mrs. Harry B. Brady (Beulah Irene)	Brady	Beulah	Irene
Mrs. Robert T. Larsen (Marion Dee)	Larsen	Marion	Dee
Mrs. Robert T. Larson (Marion)	Larson	Marion	

Names Involving Indexing Rules 17, 18, 19, and 20 As They Should Be Typed on File Cards and Sequenced

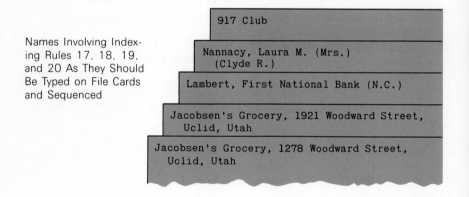

```
917 Club

Nannacy, Laura M. (Mrs.)
   (Clyde R.)

Lambert, First National Bank (N.C.)

Jacobsen's Grocery, 1921 Woodward Street,
   Uclid, Utah

Jacobsen's Grocery, 1278 Woodward Street,
   Uclid, Utah
```

Filing Practice

Complete Job 9 in the practice set or refer to the Appendix for practice exercises.

Variations in Alphabetic Indexing Rules

You now have had considerable practice in applying the twenty alphabetic indexing rules. These rules are applied in practically every office throughout the United States. Just as a typist can change from one make of typewriter to another because the keyboard is standard, so can you adjust readily to the filing system used wherever you might work.

Occasionally it is necessary to depart slightly from one or more of the indexing rules in order to provide for the special needs of a business. Variations from the standard rules should be kept to the minimum; but once a variation is adopted, it should be followed consistently by everyone in the firm.

Cross-Referencing

A record should always be filed under the caption by which it is most likely to be requested. Occasionally a record will be requested by a caption that is different from that under which it was filed. For instance, imagine that you receive a letter from Jones and Parker pertaining to a contract that your company has with Paul Smith, a building contractor. You decide that the letter is most likely to be called for under *Jones and Parker,* so this is where it is filed. However, because the letter also may be asked for under the name *Paul Smith,* a reference card or sheet should be filed under the caption *Smith,*

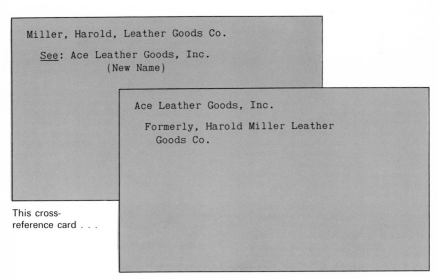

```
Miller, Harold, Leather Goods Co.

    See: Ace Leather Goods, Inc.
         (New Name)
```

```
Ace Leather Goods, Inc.

    Formerly, Harold Miller Leather
    Goods Co.
```

This cross-reference card . . . refers to this index card.

Paul. This procedure is known as *cross-referencing.* The file worker should cross-reference whenever there is a possibility that a record might be requested under more than one name.

Note the following principles of cross-referencing.

1. When it is more likely that a firm or an institution record will be asked for under a word other than the first indexing unit, the record is cross-referenced under that word.

FILED UNDER	CROSS-REFERENCE
Committee for Rehabilitation	Rehabilitation, Committee for
Imperial Lodge	Lodge Imperial
University of Woodlands	Woodlands University

CROSS-REFERENCE SHEET

Name or Subject
    Bicycle Tires

Date
4/12/19--

Regarding
    Adaptability

SEE

Name or Subject
    Automobile Tires
    Center Garage
    124 Cleaver St.
    Nashville, Tenn. 37210

File cross-reference sheet under name or subject at top of the sheet and by the latest date of papers. Describe matter for identification purposes. The papers themselves should be filed under name or subject after "SEE."

Made in U.S.A

2. It is sometimes difficult to decide which part of an individual's name is the surname. In such cases, index the name as normally written and cross-reference under a transposition of the name.

FILED UNDER	CROSS-REFERENCE
Frank, Henry	Henry, Frank
Bryan, Charles	Charles, Bryan
Alton, James	James, Alton

3. Some organizations are better known by initials than by their complete names. Material, however, should be filed under the complete name and a cross-reference made under the abbreviated version. Acronyms (words formed from initials) are also handled in this manner.

FILED UNDER	CROSS-REFERENCE
Future Business Leaders of America	FBLA
National Business Education Association	NBEA
Volunteers in Service to America	VISTA

4. When a record is likely to be called for most frequently by subject, with an occasional request by name of individual or company, it should be filed under the subject caption with cross-reference made under the individual's or company's name.

FILED UNDER	CROSS-REFERENCE
Bond Papers (information concerning samples of bond papers)	Willamette Printers (name of firm from which most bond paper is purchased)
Taxation	Committee for Civic Improvement

5. Some firm names contain spellings that are contrary to the dictionary spelling of the words. In such cases, records should be filed under the unusual spelling and cross-referenced under the dictionary spelling.

FILED UNDER	CROSS-REFERENCE
Brite-Clean Laundry	Bright-Clean Laundry
Rite Mix Flour Company	Right Mix Flour Company
X-R-Sizer Studios	Exerciser Studios

Filing Practice

Refer to Jobs 10–17 in the practice set or refer to the Appendix for practice exercises.

Alphabetizing in Telephone Directories

The basic rules for indexing are generally followed by telephone companies in compiling their directories. However, certain exceptions to the twenty

indexing rules presented in this chapter are observed for most directory listings.   So that the students of office procedures will be able to locate telephone
numbers quickly, the most important of these exceptions are presented here.

1. To meet common reference habits, at the customer's request, a complete individual name that is the first part of a firm name may be
   listed under the first name rather than the surname.

   Arthur Murray Studios (may be listed under "A")

   B. Altman and Co. (may be listed under "B")

   Henry Ford Hospital (may be listed under "H")

2. Names that are spelled either as one or as two words are treated as
   spelled by the customer.

   North Side Theater (3 units)

   > *precedes*

   Northside Market (2 units)

3. Single letters other than abbreviations are considered as separate
   indexing units.   However, groups of single letters at the beginning
   of a firm name are treated independently of the rest of the name,
   and the "nothing comes before something" rule applies for such
   groups.

   AA Brick Company *precedes* AAA Glass Company

4. Organizations with numbers in their titles, such as unions, lodges, and
   clubs, are arranged in numerical sequence if the listings are alphabetically the same up to the numbers.   These listings *follow* all other
   listings that are the same up to the number.

   Local Variety Store *precedes* Local 28 ILGWU

   Local 28 ILGWU *precedes* Local 93 ILGWU

5. The letter *s* after an apostrophe (Carter's) *is* considered in alphabetizing for a directory listing.

   Brooks Jewelry *precedes* Brook's Laundry

6. The articles *a, an,* and *the* are considered the same as any other word.
   When *The* is the first word of a firm name it may be dropped, placed
   at the end of the firm name, or, at the customer's request, left at the
   beginning of the name.

   A Better Candy Company (listed under "A")

   The Gift Mart (listed under "G" as "Gift Mart, The" or listed under
   "T" as "The Gift Mart" if customer requests)

7. Prepositions (*by, for, of,* etc.) are considered the same as any other
   word.

   Stevens of Townsend *precedes* Stevens Pharmacy

8. Conjunctions (*or, as*) other than *and* are considered the same as any
   other word.   (The conjunction *and,* usually listed as *&,* is not considered in indexing.)

   Mick-or-Ralph Stores *precedes* Mick Plumbing Supply

Indexing Review

A. What is the *first* indexing unit in each of these names?

1. Lennox Air Conditioning
2. Gazette-Times
3. Dr. Pepper
4. KFLY Broadcast Station
5. Adam's Gas & Supplies
6. West Side Nursery
7. West Hill Branch, U. S. Nat'l Bank, Reedsport, Mich.
8. Mrs. Selma Harter
9. 49th Street Market
10. Van Waggoner Music Shop
11. Army and Navy Tailors
12. Humphrey Elden Sign Shop
13. Nat. Cash Register Co.
14. M. E. Woodstock & Sons
15. Dr. Pepper Bottling Co.
16. Adams' Fur Salon

B. What is the *second* indexing unit in each of these names?

1. Mock's Mercury Motors
2. Houston, Thomas & Johnson
3. Porter-Murphy Distillers
4. De Witt's Radiator Repair
5. Bee Hive Truck & Auto Rental
6. Mrs. Fred Perkins (Mary K.)
7. Mid West Growers, Inc.
8. Harold Nelson Life Ins.
9. D & B Motor Co.
10. Uptown Barber Shop
11. Junction 319
12. Wellsher Salon of Beauty
13. Burton Wilhelm's Shell Serv.
14. New Jersey Field & Stream
15. Father Riley
16. Clarence Bradford-Hyatt

C. Which of these groups of names are properly alphabetized?

1. Janitorial Service Co.
   Janitor's Supply, Inc.
   Janitors' Club
2. Coleman Jewelers
   John Coleman
   Larry Colman
3. Helen Meier-Schmidt
   Meier-Schmidt Rug Co.
   The Meier-Schmidt Scholarship
4. Charnholm's Hardware, Corvallis, Oreg.
   Charnholm's Hardware, Cornwallis, Nev.
   Charnholm's Hardware, Cornelius, Nev.
5. Denson Feed and Seed
   Fred Denson and Sons
   The James Denson Station
6. Jim the Fixer
   Jim Flack
   Jim and John Garage
7. Willer's Motel & Apts.
   Willers' Motel & Garage
   Morris Willers & Sons
8. First Federal Savings & Loan, Monroe, Oregon
   First Federal Savings & Loan, Monroe, Texas
   First Federal Savings & Loan, Monro, Washington

D. Alphabetize the names in each of the following groups.

1. Plastic Material and Supplies
   Jim Plover's Plastics
   Plunket the Plastics Man
   Plastics, Inc.

2. Dr. James S. Riley
   Jas. Riley, Consultant
   The Riley-James Fund
   Jos. Riley-James

3. Starr Plumbing and Heating
   Starr-Plumber School
   Mrs. Philip Starr (Mary V.)
   Star Trading Center

4. McCulloch Clinic
   Clarence McCulloch
   The MacCulloch Coach Co.
   U. S. National Bank, McCloud, Miss.

5. Inter-State Insurance Co.
   Inter-State Investors Co.
   Interstate Geographic Survey
   Inter-Ocean Fisheries

6. Jensen's
   Jensen Paint Co.
   P. L. Jensen & Son
   The Jensen House

7. Marvin G. Paasche
   Passche the Magician
   M. A. Paschee
   Professor O. Paasche

8. U. S. Dept. of Marine Biology
   Department of Finance, Uruguay
   U. S. Marine Products Co.
   United States Secretary of State

9. Mrs. Richard Newton
   (Judith Ann)
   The Newton Jewelers
   The J. W. Newton Co.
   Newton-Jones, Ltd.

10. 4th Street Salon
    Sam Forsyth & Son
    40 and 4 Club
    Fornier Consultants

11. James Gathercoal, Architect
    Gathercoal the Architect
    Clara Gaten-Olson
    The Gaten-Olson Mill

12. Brazil Nut Exporters
    Republic of Brazil, Sec. of
      the Navy
    The Brazil Commission, Inc.
    Natalie Brazill

Questions and Problems

1. Why are standardized rules for filing needed?
2. Explain the meaning of *indexing* in the filing process.
3. Define the following terms as used in this chapter: (a) *unit*, (b) *alphabetizing*, (c) *surname*, (d) *given name*, and (e) *complete individual name*.
4. Describe clearly how comparisons are made between first units of names to be indexed, then second units, etc.
5. Explain the need for cross-referencing.
6. What is a surname prefix? How is it indexed?
7. What is a caption?
8. Describe how names are typed on cards for indexing.
9. Describe the punctuation you prefer for names on cards. Why?
10. Can you devise an easy way to remember when hyphenated names should be considered as one unit? as two units?
11. Compound geographic names are sometimes considered as one unit, sometimes as two units. Why?
12. Give the two possible combinations for a married woman's legal name.
13. Why might an office have to deviate from the standard filing rules?

Case Problems in Records Management

1. William Blair asked his brother to help him with homework involving the indexing rules. The brother, who worked in a small neighborhood real estate office, remarked that he did not bother with the indexing rules, because he was the only one who used the files. William said that he thought all file workers should use standard indexing rules. What is your opinion?

2. Ann Collins works in the filing department of a company specializing in hotel supplies. Recently she remarked to her supervisor that in her filing work there were too many names in which the first indexing unit was "Hotel." Her superior suggested Ann use some other unit in the names as the first unit. Although Ann did not say so to her supervisor, she thought it would be incorrect. What do you think about the superior's suggestion?

3. Bert Clark, a new worker in the sales department of a textbook publishing company, remarked to a fellow worker that he thinks the practice of making out two cards for the customer files—one for the name of a school and one for its principal—is unnecessary double work. His fellow worker disagreed. What do you think?

3 Managing General Correspondence

WRITTEN CORRESPONDENCE is the keystone of communications for American business. A large insurance firm depends almost entirely upon the written word to communicate with the thousands of people with whom it deals. The same is true of the magazine publisher, the mail-order house, and the government agency. Hotels, department stores, banks, and travel agencies also carry on large volumes of correspondence. Of course, the amount of correspondence sent and received varies according to the size of the organization and the kind of business in which it is engaged. In all organizations, however, it is important that the correspondence and other records be managed so that they can be readily referred to when business transactions require the use of the information.

Definition of Correspondence

Any written communication that is not intended to be placed in a card or forms file is considered to be *correspondence*. Correspondence may be classified according to its source as incoming, outgoing, or internal.

Incoming correspondence includes such communications received from outside the organization as letters, contracts, telegrams, reports, and applications.

Outgoing correspondence includes such communications sent to individuals or companies outside the organization as letters, telegrams, and inquiries.

It is customary to retain for the files at least one carbon copy or photocopy of each item of outgoing correspondence.

Internal correspondence includes such written communications between departments in the same organization as memos, reports, and notices.

Organization of Correspondence

To ensure convenient reference, it is important that an organization keep related records together. For example, the carbon copy of a reply to Bradley, Incorporated should be filed in the same place as the incoming letter from Bradley that prompted the reply. If an interoffice memorandum is written regarding the same incoming letter, the memorandum, too, should be stored with it. Most likely, later correspondence to, from, or about Bradley, Incorporated will also be kept in the same place.

How the correspondence is organized—the type of system and the captions used—will depend on the information needed by the business. A doctor is primarily interested in data about his patients. Therefore, he would use an alphabetic system; the captions would be the names of his patients, and all records pertaining to any one patient would be stored together. However, a purchasing agent, who is responsible for the buying of hundreds of products, would be primarily interested in the items being purchased. Therefore, he would use a subject system; the captions would be names of products, and all records pertaining to any one item—for example, transistors—would be stored together.

Vertical Filing

Many years ago, papers were stored by piling one on top of the other in "book" fashion. Sometimes they were impaled on a sharp metal spike or spindle. Small wonder that it was difficult to find and remove a needed paper, especially if it were near the bottom of the stack! When papers were stored horizontally, the records became "dog-eared," unattractive, and often illegible. Thus, vertical filing—standing papers on end, supported by guides and folders—came about. In addition to keeping records in better condition, vertical filing permits easier and faster handling of each paper and requires less space.

Housing Records

There are many types of storage equipment for correspondence. Ready-made files are available from office equipment manufacturers to house records of almost every shape and description. Descriptions of several kinds of filing equipment are given in Chapter 9.

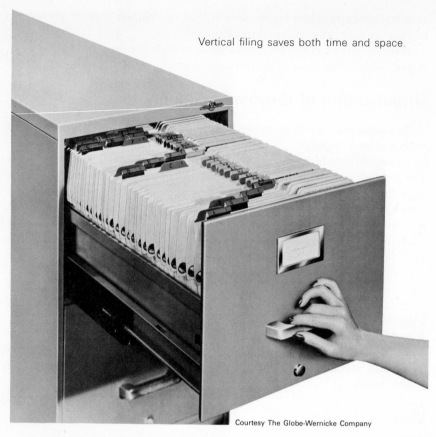

Vertical filing saves both time and space.

Courtesy The Globe-Wernicke Company

The most common storage container for correspondence is the familiar drawer-type metal filing cabinet. Open-shelf files are also extensively used for the storage of correspondence.

File Drawer Labels

In order that its contents can be identified quickly, each file drawer should be properly labeled. On the front of each file drawer is a holder for the drawer label. The caption on the label indicates the alphabetic limitations of the records housed there. Suppose the drawer contains correspondence that begins with the name *Dabney* and ends with the name *Furman*. The label or caption can be one of two types: (1) *single-caption*—single letter *D* indicating where in the alphabet the records begin, or (2) *double*, or *closed*, *caption*—the two letters *D* and *F* separated by a hyphen (*D-F*) or placed in vertical arrangement (*D* to *F*) to indicate where the alphabetic sequence begins and ends.

Open-Shelf Files Used for the Storage of Correspondence

File Guides

Guides—cardboard or pressboard sheets—in a correspondence file serve two purposes:

1. They separate the file drawer into distinct, labeled *sections* and make it easy to locate specific records.

2. They support the records in the drawer and prevent them from bowing or sagging.

Extending above the top edge of a correspondence guide is a tab, which identifies the alphabetic range of the records to be stored behind it. Guides

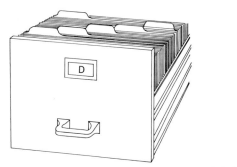
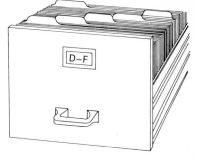

File Drawers with Single Caption Label (Left) and Double Caption Label (Right)

are somewhat larger than the file folders and are described by the width of the tab (commonly called *cut*). A *one-fifth cut* means that the tab extends along one-fifth of the top edge of the guide. A *one-third cut* means that the tab occupies one-third of the guide's top edge, and so on. A tab occupying the first one-fifth on the left edge of the guide as you face the file is said to be in *first position;* the second tab in the second one-fifth from the left, *second position;* the third tab from the left, *third position;* and so on. Guides are said to be in a staggered arrangement when their tabs are in successive positions reading left to right. Guides are commonly available in various cuts ranging from one-half to one-fifth.

Guide captions, which are the titles on guide tabs, identify the records filed behind the guides. Some guide tabs have the captions printed directly on them. Other tabs are of the holder type, metal or plastic, into which can be inserted a small strip on which the caption has been typed or printed.

Guide captions may be single or double, as in the case of the file drawer labels. They should be kept short so that they can be read quickly and easily. Single captions indicate where each section begins. The records to be filed after a single caption are those beginning with the caption on the guide tab up to, but not including, the caption on the next guide tab. The use of single guide captions makes expansion in the file easy, because additional guides can be inserted wherever another subdivision is needed. Single captions may also

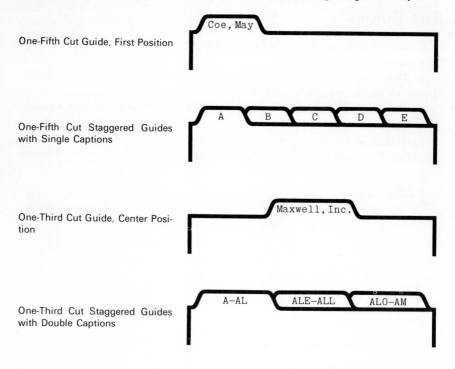

One-Fifth Cut Guide, First Position

One-Fifth Cut Staggered Guides with Single Captions

One-Third Cut Guide, Center Position

One-Third Cut Staggered Guides with Double Captions

be easier to read than double captions, because they can be larger and more legible on the tabs. The advantage of the double caption is that it shows the entire range of the section covered by the guide.

The number of guides needed in a file will be determined largely by the needs of the office. Normally, each file drawer will contain from 20 to 40 guides in order to facilitate reference and provide support for the folders.

Guides are available in sets ranging from 25 for use in the very small business to 200,000 for use in the very large organization. The captions may be preprinted on the tabs, or they can be inserted into the metal or plastic caption holders fastened to the top edge of the guide. Removable caption guides more readily permit rearrangement of tab captions.

File Folders

File folders serve as containers for correspondence in the file drawers. They are made of heavy paper that is folded so that all or part of the top edge of the back extends one-half inch or more above the front. At the bottom front of the folder are several horizontal scores, or creases, that permit expansion of the folder as up to 100 sheets of correspondence are added.

A projecting tab on the back edge of the folder provides a place for the title, or caption, of the folder contents. The caption is usually typed on a folder label, and the label is attached to the tab.

Folders, like file guides, are available with tabs of various widths, or cuts. Furthermore, folders can be obtained with tabs in any one of several positions along the top edge of the folder.

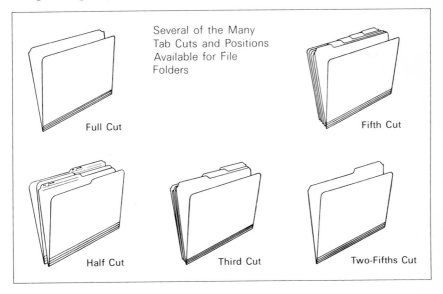

Several of the Many
Tab Cuts and Positions
Available for File
Folders

Full Cut

Fifth Cut

Half Cut

Third Cut

Two-Fifths Cut

Right

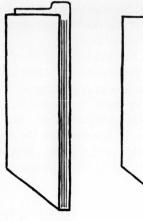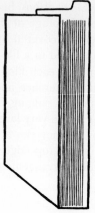

25 Sheets
(First Score Broken)

100 Sheets
(Maximum)

More Than 100 Sheets
(New Folder Required)

Wrong

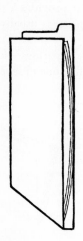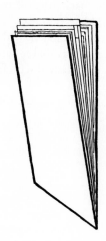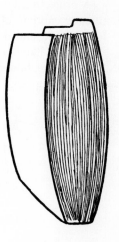

Papers curl if scores
are broken too soon.

And they ride up if
scores are not
broken soon enough.

But even when scores
are broken, place no
more than 100
sheets
in a standard folder.

Right and Wrong Methods for Using File Folder Scores

Preparation of Folder Labels

Gummed labels for folder captions, about four inches wide, are available in perforated strips, in adhesive strips, or in continuous rolls. Each kind of label is obtainable in a variety of colors. Remember the following suggestions and illustrations when you prepare folder labels:

1. Some labels are folded into a front and a back portion. The wider portion, if one is wider, is always the front of the label and is the one on which the caption is typed. Start typing the caption on the third space in from the left edge of the label and on the second line below the crease. The caption should be started at the same place on every folder label, and the label should be affixed in the same place on every tab. Thus, all first words on tabs of like position will be in a straight line when they are placed in a file drawer. This makes for greater ease in reading, facilitates finding, and improves appearance.

2. The words or the items of the caption are typed in indexing order.

3. In some offices, the entire first line of a label is capitalized; in others, only the first letter of each important word. The latter style is preferable; however, whichever style is adopted should be used consistently on all the labels.

4. In some offices, punctuation, including the period after abbreviations, is omitted entirely. Instead, two spaces are left where the punctuation would have been. Other offices use normal punctuation.

5. Block style is preferred if the caption includes more than one item. If any item in the caption runs over to a second line, its runover should be indented three spaces in order to identify that part with the line above.

Aligning Folder Captions

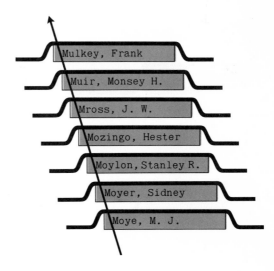

The typed label (1) is de-
tached at the perforation (2),
moistened and folded at the
center crease (3), and attached to the tab of the
file folder (4).

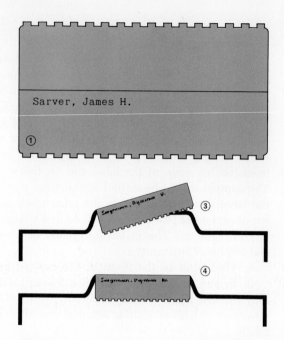

Sarver, James H.

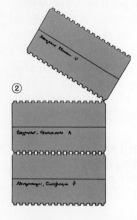

High-speed data processing equipment is now being used for the printing
of captions onto long strips of adhesive file labels and for printing captions
directly onto the tabs of long strips of folders. The folders are separated at
perforations after printing. They are designed for large or constantly changing files with a relatively short lifetime.

File Drawer Capacity

The usable space in most correspondence file drawers is about 26 inches—
front to back. Maximum capacity is approximately 5,000 papers, including

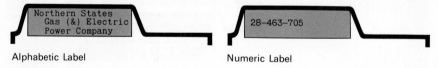

Northern States
Gas (&) Electric
Power Company

Alphabetic Label

28–463–705

Numeric Label

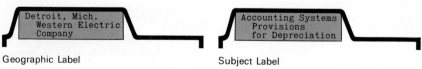

Detroit, Mich.
Western Electric
Company

Geographic Label

Accounting Systems
Provisions
for Depreciation

Subject Label

Folder Labels for Different Filing Systems

Courtesy Remington Rand

These adhesive file labels are printed at high speed on data processing equipment.

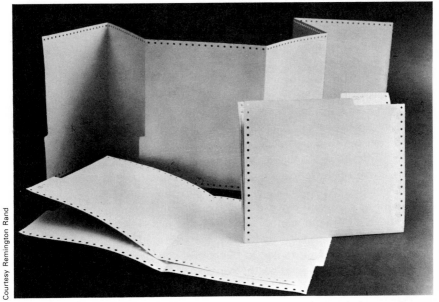

Courtesy Remington Rand

These marginal-hole punched folders require no labels because the captions are printed directly onto the tabs by means of high-speed data processing equipment.

the necessary guides and folders. For more efficient operation, however, it is best not to place more than approximately 4,000 pieces in each file drawer as tight packing makes it difficult for folders or papers to be removed and inserted.

Importance of a Collection Routine

Records management begins long before materials are placed in the files. In the first place, a definite routine should be established for collecting and assembling papers that are important enough to be kept. Haphazard collection procedures are certain to cause delays in getting needed records to the files in time for them to be of the most use.

Correspondence to be placed in the files should not be permitted to accumulate for long periods of time on desks, in desk trays, and in desk drawers. It should be filed as quickly as possible after the transaction involving the record has been completed. Most organizations have fixed policies governing the filing of records. These policies are especially important in a large organization where perhaps thousands of pieces of correspondence are handled every day and where the work of hundreds of people is affected by the availability of records.

Receiving Correspondence

The procedure for handling incoming correspondence varies somewhat among companies, even among those of comparable size. In most large organizations, there is usually a central mail department, which has the responsibility for sorting all incoming mail and delivering it to the appropriate individuals or departments. Letters addressed to individual executives are delivered unopened, and their respective secretaries open the mail (except those envelopes marked "personal") and read it. Letters not addressed to specific persons or departments must be opened by the central mail department in order to determine to whom the correspondence is to be delivered.

In a small organization the procedure is similar; however, in place of a central mailing department, more likely only one employee, such as the receptionist or a general office worker, handles all incoming mail.

Whoever opens the mail should check first to see that the return address is on the correspondence. If it is not, the return address should be clipped from the envelope and stapled to the correspondence. The person opening the mail should also stamp on the correspondence the date it was received. Some companies require that the time of day also be stamped. One purpose of date-stamping is to fix responsibility for delays in the delivery of correspondence. (An incoming letter may be dated "April 15" by the writer and yet not be received until May 1.) An even more important reason for date-stamping is to provide for internal control of correspondence. Management insists that communications be handled promptly—that as little time as possible elapse between the date a communication is received and the time when definite action is taken. Where a large volume of mail is handled, automatic machines are used for opening and date-stamping mail. In smaller offices hand-operated date stamps are used.

Path of a Letter

What happens to a piece of correspondence after it is received by the mail clerk? Let's take a typical example of a letter received by Dexter and Company. When the letter is opened and date-stamped by the mail clerk, it is found to be an application for a position from a recent college graduate, William Redford. The mail clerk knows that all letters concerning employment are referred to Mr. Homer Johnston, personnel director, so the application letter is delivered to Mr. Johnston's secretary, who places it in his "in" tray or mail box. Mr. Johnston reads it. Then, with the letter in hand, he dictates a reply, inviting Mr. Redford to come in for an interview. When he is finished with Mr. Redford's letter, Mr. Johnston marks it in such a way to indicate that he is through with it and that it may be filed. This notation is referred to as a *release mark*. The release mark most commonly used is the initials of the person using a record for the first time. These initials are usually placed in the upper left corner. However, the date, some symbol, or simply a light line drawn through the contents may be used for releasing. Release marks may be handwritten or stamped (see the example on page 42). It does not matter what type of release mark Mr. Johnston chooses; it does matter, however, that he use the same mark consistently. A release mark is not necessary for carbon copies of outgoing letters and interoffice memorandums.

The secretary staples the carbon copy of Mr. Johnston's reply to the original letter from William Redford. If she keeps the personnel files for Mr. Johnston, she places the correspondence in her "to be filed" folder. If the files are maintained by a staff of filing specialists, she places the correspondence in her "out" basket.

Special folders or some other means should be used to identify for the collecting messenger which of the accumulated material in the out basket is to be routed to the mail department and which is to be sent to the file department.

It is important to remember that not all items of incoming correspondence or carbon copies of outgoing correspondence need to be filed. Many routine acknowledgments or relatively unimportant communications are discarded after they have been read or answered. The decision of whether or not to file should be made by the executive who handles the correspondence.

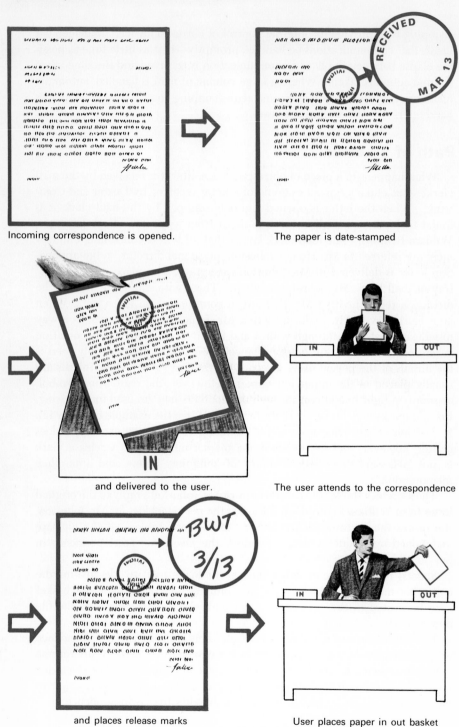

Incoming correspondence is opened.

The paper is date-stamped

and delivered to the user.

The user attends to the correspondence

and places release marks
on papers to be filed.

User places paper in out basket
for delivery to files.

Path of a Letter from Receipt to Release for Filing

Steps in the Filing Process

After correspondence has been released for filing, it travels through five distinct steps: (1) inspecting, (2) indexing, (3) coding, (4) sorting, and (5) storing. These steps are illustrated in chart form on page 45. Whether the filing is done by the specialized worker in the centralized filing department or by the secretary in a small office, all the steps must be performed to some degree.

Step 1: Inspecting. It is important, especially in larger filing installations, that each piece of correspondence be scanned for a release mark before it is filed. This is the first step in the filing process; the release mark is the authority to file. If a paper should reach the file worker without the release mark, it is customary to return it to the person to whom it had been assigned.

Step 2: Indexing. Indexing, you will remember, is the mental process by which you determine the name, subject, or other caption under which a piece of correspondence is to be filed.

There are at least five different clues for determining the caption under which a piece of correspondence is to be placed:

a. Name contained in the letterhead (incoming correspondence)
b. Name of the person or organization addressed (carbon copy of outgoing correspondence)
c. Name in the signature (incoming correspondence)
d. Name of subject discussed in the correspondence (incoming or outgoing correspondence)
e. Name of a geographic location about which the correspondence is concerned (incoming or outgoing correspondence)

Correspondence should be indexed under the caption by which it is most likely to be requested from the files. Whenever a paper may be called for in several ways, it should be filed under the most frequently used caption and cross-referenced under the others. You will recall that cross-referencing means placing a sheet of paper containing information about the actual location of a document, or a photocopy of the document itself, in all places in a file where a person might look for it.

Step 3: Coding. Indexing is the mental process of determining the caption under which the correspondence is to be filed. Writing or otherwise indicating that caption on the correspondence is known as *coding*. There are three common methods of coding correspondence for alphabetic systems:

a. The caption, or name to be indexed, can be underlined. A colored pencil is preferable.

b. If the caption under which the correspondence should be filed is not mentioned in the body of the message or does not appear anywhere on the paper, that caption is written in the upper right corner.

c. If it is necessary to cross-reference the piece of correspondence, the caption under which it is actually to be placed in the file should be underlined or written, as explained in *a* and *b*. The caption selected for the cross-reference should also be underlined or written, and in addition, an X should be placed at the end of the line or after the written caption to indicate that it is a cross-reference. Examine the coded letter on page 45.

The code, then, is the silent sentinel that gives direction, exactness, and speed to the initial trip of the correspondence to the files, as well as the return trips to the files after requests for its use.

Step 4: Sorting. Sorting is the process of arranging the records in alphabetic order after they have been coded. This speeds up the process of placing correspondence in the files.

What would happen if, in an organization where the volume of correspondence is heavy, papers were taken to the files without first having been sorted? It is unlikely that the individual pieces would be in the proper sequence for placement in the files. This would result in a great deal of lost motion—backtracking over and over again to the same folders.

In many offices desk-top sorting is adequate. It is done in the following manner:

a. First, the papers are sorted into a small number of piles according to convenient divisions, such as *A–C, D–G, H–L, M–R,* and *S–Z.*

b. Next, the pieces are alphabetized within each division. The first pile would be re-sorted according to the *A*'s, *B*'s, and *C*'s—thus becoming *three* piles if all three letters of the alphabet were represented. The next alphabetic combination, *D–G,* could have four piles; *H–L,* five; and so on.

c. The correspondence in pile *A* is further alphabetized so that *Adams, A.* comes before *Adams, C.,* and so that *Anderson, Carl* is placed after *Adams, C.,* etc. The *B* and *C* piles are given the same treatment.

d. Finally, the three *A–C* piles are placed in alphabetic sequence—*B* on top of *C* and *A* on top of *B.* After this step is repeated for the remaining combinations, the correspondence is ready to be filed. If sorting space is limited, it may be decided to store the *A–C* group in the files before repeating the sorting routine for the other alphabetic divisions.

In offices where there is a large volume of correspondence to be readied for the files, special sorting devices and equipment are used to simplify and

STEPS IN CORRESPONDENCE FILING

1. Inspecting. Correspondence is checked to make sure it has been released for filing.

2. Indexing. The name by which correspondence will most likely be requested from the files is determined. In this example it was decided that *The David Harris Company* would be the caption under which the letter would be filed.

3. Coding. The caption determined in the indexing step is underscored. The cross-reference caption is underscored, and an X is placed at the end of the line.

4. Sorting. All correspondence to be filed is alphabetized according to the underscored captions.

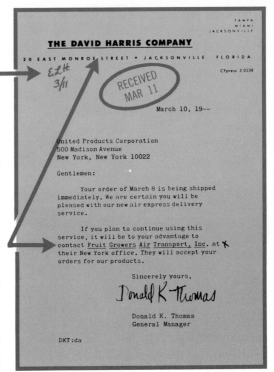

5. Storing. The papers are placed in the proper folders in the filing cabinets.

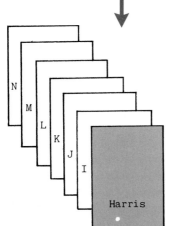

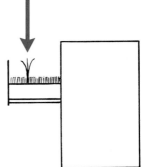

B. D. Unsworth

Sorting Correspondence for Filing

speed up sorting. There are several types from which to choose; one is shown above.

Step 5: Storing. The last step in the filing process—storing—is the actual placement of the records in the files.

Correspondence is normally stored in file folders. Here are step-by-step instructions for storing records in file folders:

a. Open the file drawer labeled by the proper alphabetic caption.
b. Using guide captions as locators, find the folder bearing the caption under which the correspondence is to be stored. Guides should be handled as much as possible from the sides so that the tabs will not become bent and the captions smudged. Even guides with metal tabs should not be used to pull the file drawer contents forward or to push them backward. It is best to straighten the contents of the file drawer occasionally by pulling the bottoms of small groups of file folders forward until they are standing upright in the drawer.
c. Raise the folder and rest it on the edge of the file drawer near the place from which it was removed.
d. Be sure that the proper folder has been removed. Compare the caption on the folder with the caption on the record being stored and with the caption on the top record already in the folder. Checking will take only a few seconds—time that may prevent many records from becoming lost.

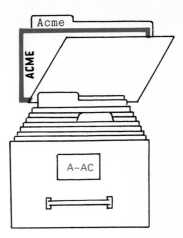

1. Find the desired folder. Lift and rest it on drawer side.

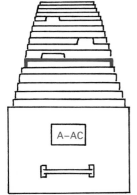

2. Compare caption on record to be filed with caption on record in folder.

3. Place record in folder with heading to the left.

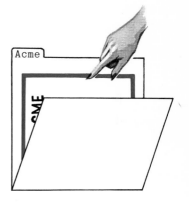

4. Carefully slide folder back to original position. Close drawer.

The Storage of Correspondence in a Drawer File

e. Place the record carefully in the folder with the *heading to the left as you face the file* so that the left side of the record will rest on the bottom of the folder. Remember that an overcrowded folder causes the contents to ride up, often covering the caption and making it difficult to handle the folder.

f. Replace the folder so that it rests on the bottom of the file drawer with its two sides in a vertical position and with the caption fully visible.

Some file workers find it practical to use the *bookmark method* of removing a file folder from its normal position. The folder is lifted, but instead of being removed completely, it is raised at one end until that end rests on the edge of the file drawer. The other lower corner either rests on the bottom of the file drawer or, because of the pressure from adjoining folders, rises somewhat higher. About one-third of the folder now is exposed above the level of the other folders in the drawer. From this position, the file worker can insert the piece of correspondence in the folder and return it to its proper location. The bookmark method has the advantage of maintaining the folder's proper position in the file, thereby saving time.

Questions and Problems

1. What is *correspondence?*
2. Distinguish among incoming, outgoing, and internal correspondence.
3. Why is it important that correspondence from one individual or organization be stored together?
4. Why is vertical filing superior to piling up papers in book fashion?
5. Describe single- and double-caption file drawer labels.
6. What purposes are served by file drawer guides?
7. Describe what is meant by each of these terms: tab, cut, one-third cut, position, staggered arrangement.
8. Why should guide captions be kept short?
9. Tell why the use of single guide captions makes expansion easy in the file.
10. Discuss the advantage of double, or closed, captions over single captions.
11. What generally determines the number of guides in each file drawer?
12. Why is it important to have a definite procedure for collecting papers to be filed?
13. Name some examples of types of correspondence that might be discarded rather than filed.
14. Why is it important to know when correspondence was received?
15. What is the purpose of a release mark?
16. Describe the steps in correspondence filing.
17. Distinguish between indexing and coding.

18. When should a piece of correspondence be cross-referenced?
19. Why should folders not be overcrowded?
20. If there is a full-sized file available, demonstrate how to remove a folder from the file drawer, insert a paper, and return the folder to its place.

Case Problems in Records Management

1. Jack Miller is reorganizing the files for a garage he just purchased. The file drawers do not have guides, and as an economy measure, Jack intends to do without them. Instead he is going to place a folder with the appropriate caption in front of each alphabetic division to serve as a guide. Do you think his plan is wise? Why?
2. The Barry Steel Company, which owns 6 manufacturing plants and 18 distribution centers, has a considerable amount of interoffice correspondence. This correspondence pertains not only to intercompany activities but to customers and suppliers as well. At the present time interoffice correspondence is separated from all other records and stored in separate file cabinets. Do you approve of this procedure?
3. Jack Hastings, the shop foreman of the Paxton Tool and Die Company, keeps records referred to him on spindle files. Other people using those records complain they are difficult to refer to and that the spike sometimes obliterates information. Jack says it is necessary to handle the records in this fashion to keep them from blowing away. What would you suggest to improve the situation?
4. Mr. Carroll is the proprietor of a small hardware store that sells on both a cash and a credit basis. He does not have a file cabinet but keeps all records in the drawers of his desk. He doesn't use file folders either but fastens related records together with paper clips. What do you think of the system that he is now using?
5. Henry Addams decides to eliminate coding and to proceed directly from indexing to sorting. He thinks this will save time in filing. Do you agree?
6. Helen Lane works in a file department that has its files in a row along a 50-foot wall. The A file is on the left and the Z is on the right. Her desk is next to the A file. Because she has only four letters to file, she decides not to sort them. The letters are in this order: one from John Zimmer is on top, next is one from Peter Adams, then comes one from the Zenith Box Company, and on the bottom is one from Allen Suppliers. If she had sorted these papers, approximately how much walking would she have eliminated?
7. An office practice class of 20 receives 2,000 schedule cards to be alphabetized by names of students. How would you organize the class to get this job done in minimum time?

Managing Card
Records and
Business Forms

As you learned in Chapter 3, correspondence includes such types of written communications as letters, reports, and telegrams. Equally important for business operation are the numerous card records and business forms used for recording and communicating day-to-day business information. Examples of card records are address files, inventory records, and customer accounts. Examples of business forms are purchase orders, invoices, checks, and sales slips. Just as correspondence must be properly managed for efficient use, card records and business forms must be created, stored, and used according to principles of good records management.

Card Records

Card records are distinguished from correspondence in two ways: (1) they are relatively small sheets of pressboard instead of large sheets of paper, and (2) they are not kept in folders as is correspondence. Card files are used both as indexes to correspondence filing systems and as independent records.

As an organizer of information, a card file has certain advantages over a list kept in a notebook:

1. Information can be inserted easily by the preparation of a new card.

2. Information can be deleted quickly by the destruction of an old card.

3. Information can be rearranged in any sequence—alphabetic, geographic, numeric, or subject.

50

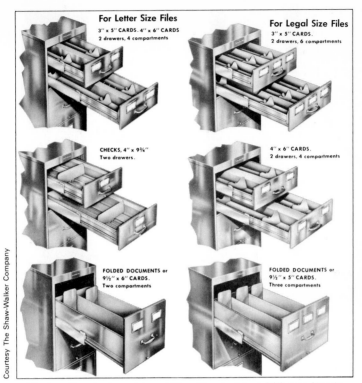

For Letter Size Files
3" x 5" CARDS. 4" x 6" CARDS
2 drawers, 4 compartments

For Legal Size Files
3" x 5" CARDS.
2 drawers, 6 compartments

CHECKS, 4" x 9¾"
Two drawers.

4" x 6" CARDS.
2 drawers, 4 compartments

FOLDED DOCUMENTS or
9½" x 6" CARDS.
Two compartments

FOLDED DOCUMENTS or
9½" x 5" CARDS.
Three compartments

Courtesy The Shaw-Walker Company

Varying Standard- and Legal-Size Files to Meet Different Needs

4. A group of cards can be referred to by several workers simultaneously. However, most lists are so compact that only one worker can refer to them at a time.

5. Certain kinds of cards can be placed in certain business machines for sorting, posting of data, and processing.

Card filing is used in business whenever there is a large number of products, customers, facts and figures, or other items to be referred to. For example, many firms have card files in their purchasing departments. On the cards in these files are names of suppliers and purchases made from them. Sales records also are kept on cards, and from them management can easily determine sales volume according to territory, product, department, or salesman. The cards need only to be reshuffled to produce various categories of information. Inventory records are kept on cards so that records about new products can easily be added, records about discontinued products can be removed, and the quantity of a product on hand can be kept up to date on an independent record.

Another common use for cards is payroll records. In such a system there is for each employee a separate card containing such information as the names

B. D. Unsworth

The rotary wheel card file is a way of keeping customers' addresses handy for immediate reference.

and ages of dependents, salary, job title, and date of employment. Sometimes customer accounts are kept on cards that are placed in a machine for daily posting of both sales and receipts. A photocopy of the card may be sent to the customer at the end of the month as a bill. And very often secretaries have card files of the names, addresses, and telephone numbers of the people their employers do business with.

Types of Card Files

All card files are classified as either *vertical*, in which cards stand upright in drawers, like correspondence, or *visible*, in which information near the edges of cards may be read without handling the cards. Either type, vertical or visible, may be organized alphabetically, numerically, geographically, by subject, or chronologically.

File workers use both vertical and visible card records for one of two purposes: to refer to existing information or to record new information. Cards that primarily provide reference are called *index card records*. For example, a secretary's address file and the index to a numeric correspondence file are both index card records. Cards on which new information is continually recorded are called *posted card records*. For example, inventory record cards for recording changes in quantities of goods in stock are posted card records.

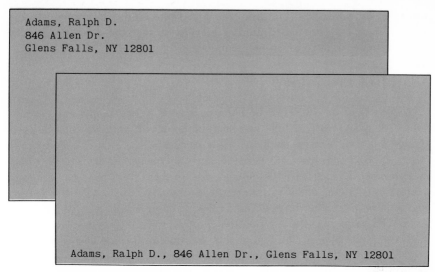

Adams, Ralph D.
846 Allen Dr.
Glens Falls, NY 12801

Adams, Ralph D., 846 Allen Dr., Glens Falls, NY 12801

The top card is for use in vertical files, the bottom for use in visible files.

Vertical Card Files

Vertical correspondence files require folders to keep related papers together and to support papers so that they will not curl and slip to the bottom of the drawer. Vertical card files, however, do not require folders because each card is an independent record containing information about *one* name, address, location, topic, or product. In addition, cards are relatively heavy, do not curl, and therefore stand quite well without much support. Otherwise, correspondence files and card files are organized in much the same way—in drawers or open cabinets with tabbed guides to speed finding and storing.

Standard sizes for vertically filed cards are 5 by 3 inches, 6 by 4 inches, and 8 by 5 inches (the first dimension is the side the card rests on when stored). Another standard card size is $7\frac{3}{8}$ by $3\frac{1}{4}$ inches. These are the dimensions of the tabulating, or punched, cards that are sorted and processed in high-speed machines. The size of a card will depend on the amount of information to be placed on it. For example, 5- by 3-inch cards are usually large enough for an address file. Customer credit records might require a 6- by 4-inch card. Job descriptions might best be kept on cards as large as 8 by 5 inches.

Regardless of the size of the cards, there should be one guide in the file drawer for each 25 to 50 cards. For faster finding, frequently referred-to vertical card files should have one guide for each 25 cards. In some vertical card files, in addition to the guides, each card has its own tab, usually bearing a number. This greatly speeds up finding when cards are constantly being removed from and inserted into the file. In most card systems, though, the cards have no tabs. When cards are prepared for storing, the caption should be typed on the second line from the top of the card. All other key data should be as close to the caption as possible so that the card can be read without being removed from its container.

Visible Card Files

If a vertical card file can be compared with a deck of playing cards in a box, then a visible card file can be compared with an open canasta hand. There is a great variety of these visible card files, more often called *visible files:* (1) horizontal trays, (2) vertical racks, (3) open bins or tubs, (4) rotary wheels, and (5) loose-leaf visible books. All of these types have an important feature in common, and it is from this feature that visible files get their name: *key information on each record can be seen without handling when the record is in storage* because the information is on a projecting edge. Thus visible files are used when it is essential that information be found rapidly. For incoming calls, the telephone operator of a company might use a visible file to find extension numbers quickly so that important customers would be talking to executives in a matter of seconds.

Visible files for posted records, such as inventories, are easy to keep up to date. With a drawer-type horizontal file tray, new inventory facts can be

Courtesy Remington Rand

This vertical card file, the Kard Veyer, contains carriers arranged in Ferris-wheel fashion. An electric motor moves the desired file into position.

quickly posted. In addition, the card never has to be removed from its holder.

Guides are not used in most visible files because each card acts as its own guide. But certain facts, such as the quantity of a product on hand, can be made to stand out by the use of *signals*—colored plastic or paper strips, tabs, or clips that can be placed on the visible portion of a card. The position or color of these signals can be used to classify, schedule, and follow up such records as inventory, sales, accounts receivable, and accounts payable. For example, the signals in the illustration on page 57 show on what months purchases of parts have been made and help ensure that purchases are kept on a regular schedule.

The requirements of the organization as to volume, location, portability, and use should determine the type of visible file to be used. Horizontal trays are well suited for posted visible records. Vertical racks are handy for quick reference to names, code numbers, and telephone numbers, while bins or tubs make excellent containers for machine-posted records. Rotary wheels provide fast reference to such information as addresses and credit data; and loose-leaf visible books, because they are portable, provide a quick reference to product information for traveling salesmen.

This automatic visible file, the Vis-U-Triever, slides one of several visible trays into posting position at the press of a button.

This vertical rotary rack for visible strip records holds a section of punched tape behind each strip.

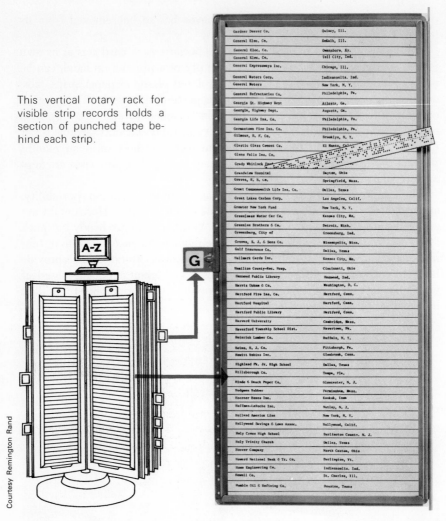

When visible record cards are being prepared, the caption should be typed as close as possible to the visible edge. Because the cards are often stored with their edges overlapping, the file worker should be certain that the caption is not obscured by another card.

Business Forms

If you were to observe 100 office employees at work at the same time, you would probably see 68 of them handling some type of business form. Forms are important carriers of business information and are the most often used kind of record in the majority of offices. They permit the recording

B. D. Unsworth

Cards in this visible file are stored horizontally in drawers. Signals have been used to ensure that purchases of parts are kept up to date.

of varying data without the recopying of information that remains constant on each form. Forms also provide uniformity in the format of data, which facilitates quick identification, filing, and finding. Every business form, such as a check, an invoice, a sales slip, an employment application, a purchase order, or a bank statement, has information printed on it. Printed data is called *static* information, such as "pay to the order of," "sold to," or "ship to." In addition, forms have blank spaces for the recording of information that varies on each form, or *variable* information. Examples of variable information include the name of the payee of a check and the address to which goods are shipped.

Most business forms are printed on paper, although many are printed on pressboard. Therefore, forms can be filed in either of two basic ways: (1) in folders, the same as correspondence, or (2) in vertical files without folders, the same as cards.

The management of business forms presents two areas of problems to the office manager. The first is how to manage business forms prior to their being filled in. The design of business forms is discussed in Chapter 12. After a form has been designed and printed, copies must be stored near the users in sufficient quantities to avoid delays. Frequently, a company will have a large variety of forms, and each form will be assigned a number. In such a case, blank forms are stored vertically in a numeric file in folders or file pockets, or horizontally on shelves. Two types of forms files are illustrated below.

The second problem area is how to organize the forms after the variable data has been added. The management of forms after they have been filled

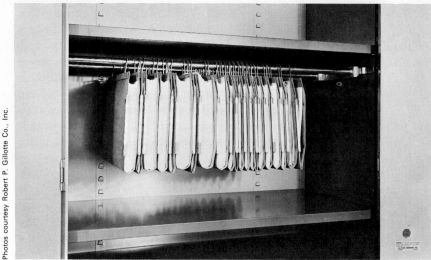

The blank forms file illustrated at the top was converted to a hanging forms file as illustrated at the bottom. Notice how much space has been saved.

in depends entirely on the business system of which the form is a part. A business system is defined as one of the administrative operations of a business, such as sales, purchases, payroll, or inventory control. Business forms and card records are the basic carriers of information for office systems. The forms and records used in business systems serve three basic purposes:

1. *As a source of input.* Every business system must have a beginning. The original record of a business event is made on some type of business record, and this original record is known as a *source document* or *source record.* For example, the original record of a sale is usually made on a sales slip (a form). The original record for a weekly payroll is usually made on a time card (a card record) for each employee. Each of these source records is a means for putting information into the system; hence the term *input* is used to describe their purpose.

2. *As a means of processing information.* The purpose of a business system is to process, or change the form of, input data so that the information will be useful in the operation of the business. Processing operations include such activities as classifying, sorting, computing, recording, summarizing, and storing. Business forms and card records that are used for recording the results of processing will be referred to as *intermediate records* in the discussion of systems that follows. For example, a customer's account (a form or card) summarizes information from sales slips (source documents) and other records. Therefore, a customer's account is an intermediate record in a sales system.

3. *As a means of output.* The results of processing are of value to the business only when they have been communicated to the proper persons for action. Transmitting processed data out of a system is referred to as *output.* Records that are used to carry data are referred to as *action records.* For example, the keeping of a customer's account is of no value to a business unless the customer eventually pays his debt. The monthly statement, which hopefully causes the customer to pay, is an action record in a sales system.

The three types of records discussed above—source records, intermediate records, and action records—cannot properly enable the system to operate unless they are organized for efficient use. When the records are not being acted upon, they must in some way be stored according to the principles of records management discussed in the remainder of this book. However, the principles of records management that are applied must first take into consideration the system of which the records are a part and how the records contribute to the operation of the system. Conversely, a plan for records management should not determine how a business system operates; rather, the requirements of a business system should determine how the records are to be managed.

The remainder of this chapter outlines the basic source, intermediate, and action records for each of several systems that are found in most business offices.

Credit Records

The purpose of a credit system is to determine to whom credit is to be granted, in what amount, and for what period of time. Credit systems are of particular importance in such retail establishments as department stores, clothing stores, and furniture stores. The success or failure of the business may depend on the currency and the accuracy of credit records. The chart below outlines source, intermediate, and action records for a typical credit system.

```
┌────────────────────────────────────────────────────────────┐
│          Source record:                                     │
│            Applications for                                 │
│              credit from                                    │
│              customers                                      │
└────────────────────────────────────────────────────────────┘
                              │
                              ▼
┌────────────────────────────────────────────────────────────┐
│        Intermediate records:                                │
│          Credit inquiries                                   │
│          Memos from credit bureau                           │
│          Credit folders or histories                        │
│          Card records for credit                            │
└────────────────────────────────────────────────────────────┘
                              │
                              ▼
┌────────────────────────────────────────────────────────────┐
│        Action records:                                      │
│          Applications for credit                            │
│            (approved or rejected)                           │
│            to sales office                                  │
│          Outgoing memos to other                            │
│            firms which have requested                       │
│            credit data on their customers                   │
└────────────────────────────────────────────────────────────┘
```

Purchases and Accounts Payable Records

The purpose of a purchases and accounts payable system is to obtain merchandise for resale or to obtain raw materials for use in manufacture and to make payment for them at the proper time. Having the proper merchandise or materials on hand at the proper time, in the needed quantity, and at a reasonable price is vital to all the operations of a merchandising or manufacturing business.

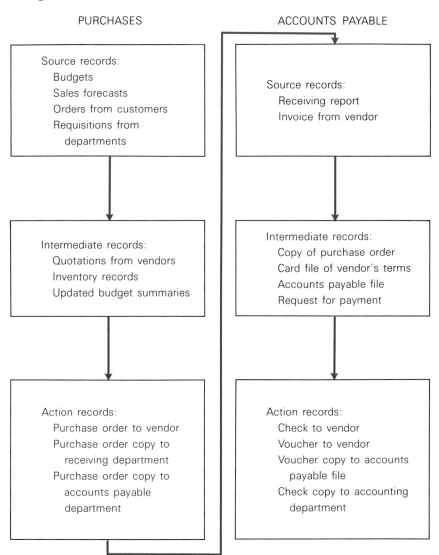

PURCHASES

Source records:
  Budgets
  Sales forecasts
  Orders from customers
  Requisitions from
    departments

Intermediate records:
  Quotations from vendors
  Inventory records
  Updated budget summaries

Action records:
  Purchase order to vendor
  Purchase order copy to
    receiving department
  Purchase order copy to
    accounts payable
    department

ACCOUNTS PAYABLE

Source records:
  Receiving report
  Invoice from vendor

Intermediate records:
  Copy of purchase order
  Card file of vendor's terms
  Accounts payable file
  Request for payment

Action records:
  Check to vendor
  Voucher to vendor
  Voucher copy to accounts
    payable file
  Check copy to accounting
    department

Shipping and Receiving Records

The purpose of a shipping and receiving system is to ensure that outgoing products are sent promptly and economically by a dependable carrier and that incoming materials are efficiently received, checked, and delivered to the using department.   In large companies the shipping and receiving functions may be performed by separate departments.   A separate shipping department is sometimes called the traffic department or office.   A shipping system, of course, is tied closely to sales, and the receiving system is closely related to purchases.

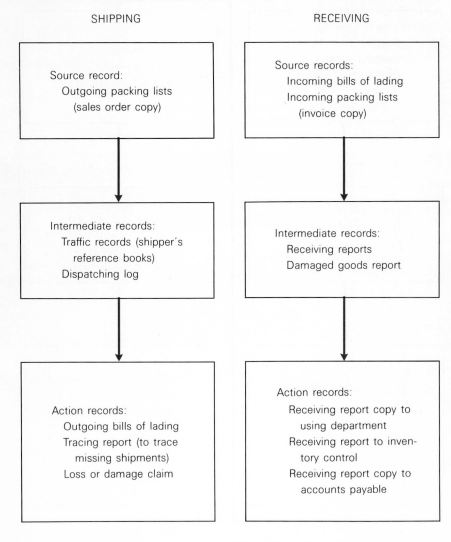

SHIPPING

RECEIVING

Source record:
  Outgoing packing lists
  (sales order copy)

Source records:
  Incoming bills of lading
  Incoming packing lists
  (invoice copy)

Intermediate records:
  Traffic records (shipper's
    reference books)
  Dispatching log

Intermediate records:
  Receiving reports
  Damaged goods report

Action records:
  Outgoing bills of lading
  Tracing report (to trace
    missing shipments)
  Loss or damage claim

Action records:
  Receiving report copy to
    using department
  Receiving report to inventory control
  Receiving report copy to
    accounts payable

Production Control Records

The purpose of production control records is to schedule the flow of raw materials with available labor and manufacturing equipment in a manufacturing firm so as to fill customer orders as promptly as possible. Production control records also serve as a source of information for determining the cost of finished products.

Source records:
    Work orders
    Production schedules

Intermediate records:
    Labor cost records
    Records of materials used
    Engineering and maintenance records

Action records:
    Finished goods records
    Inspection reports
    Completed work orders

Payroll Records

The purposes of payroll records are to assemble data for the payment of employees and to provide information for tax reports to the federal, state, and local governments.   An efficient payroll system is vital to good employer-employee relationships within any business and to meet governmental requirements for completeness and accuracy.

Source records:
    W-4 Forms (Employee's Withholding
      Exemption Certificates)
    Salary and wage schedules from personnel department
    Payroll change reports from personnel department
    Incoming punched time cards for hourly employees

Intermediate records:
    Payroll register or journal
    Employee earnings records
    Currency breakdown for cash payroll

Action records:
    Check and voucher or pay envelope to employees
    Blank time cards to check-in stations
    Reports for government, such as:
      Federal Depositary Receipt (Form 450)
      Employer's Quarterly Federal Tax Return (Form 941)
      Wage and Tax Statement (Form W-2)

Cash Records

The purpose of cash records is to ensure proper control of the money that is received and paid by a business. In all but very small firms, the overall responsibility for receiving and depositing money is assigned to one individual, and the authority and responsibility for making payments is assigned to someone else, usually an officer in another department of the business. This separation of responsibility is a double check to ensure that all funds are properly accounted for.

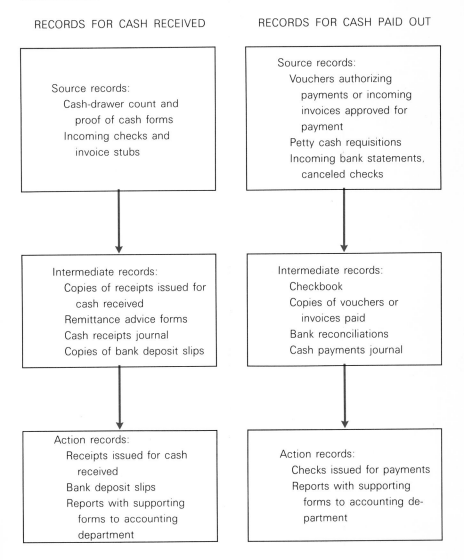

RECORDS FOR CASH RECEIVED

Source records:
Cash-drawer count and
proof of cash forms
Incoming checks and
invoice stubs

Intermediate records:
Copies of receipts issued for
cash received
Remittance advice forms
Cash receipts journal
Copies of bank deposit slips

Action records:
Receipts issued for cash
received
Bank deposit slips
Reports with supporting
forms to accounting
department

RECORDS FOR CASH PAID OUT

Source records:
Vouchers authorizing
payments or incoming
invoices approved for
payment
Petty cash requisitions
Incoming bank statements,
canceled checks

Intermediate records:
Checkbook
Copies of vouchers or
invoices paid
Bank reconciliations
Cash payments journal

Action records:
Checks issued for payments
Reports with supporting
forms to accounting de-
partment

Sales and Accounts Receivable Records

A sales system is the lifeblood of any profit-making enterprise. Without sales of goods or services, of course, the business would cease to operate. And, in the case of a business that sells on credit, the sales are of little or no value without an efficient system for the collection of accounts receivable.

SALES   ACCOUNTS RECEIVABLE

Source records:
  Sales orders
  Sales slips
  Requests for quotations

Source records:
  Filled sales orders
  Credit sales slips
  Credit memos for goods returned
  Paid invoice stubs from cashier

Intermediate records:
  Sales plans and quotas
  Microfilm records of sales slips
  Log of sales orders received
  Advertising plans and budgets

Intermediate records:
  Accounts receivable file
  Copies of outgoing invoices
  Copies of outgoing monthly
    statements

Action records:
  Quotations, price lists to
    customers
  Acknowledgments of orders
    to customers
  Sales summaries to inventory
    control department
  Orders for advertising
  Packing lists to shipping
    department

Action records:
  Invoices to customers
  Monthly statements to cus-
    tomers

Inventory Records

Inventory records provide the businessman with the information he needs in deciding what items need to be purchased in order to keep his stock of merchandise or materials at a satisfactory level. A good inventory system also reveals which items of merchandise are popular, which should be marked down for clearance, which should be promoted through advertising, and which are making the greatest profit for the business. Good inventory records are important to many of the other operations of a business: purchasing, sales, production control, and shipping and receiving, for example.

Source records:
    Receiving reports
    Sales summaries
    Summaries of sales returns
    Summaries of returns of purchases

Intermediate records:
    Stock records (perpetual inventory of goods on hand)
    Style books (information on color, sizes of items in stock)
    Records of physical inventory count

Action records:
    Inventory listings to management and buyers
    Low stock reports to purchasing department

Other Types of Records

Some business records are of such size, shape, or weight that their storage calls for special equipment or for changes in the usual correspondence, card, or forms filing procedures. The following list gives only a few of the many unique types of records that must be filed in business:

Blueprints	Maps
Books	Microfilms and filmstrips
Catalogs	Motion picture films
Certificates and licenses	Pamphlets
Clippings	Phonograph records
Drawings	Photographs
Financial statements	Printing cuts
Legal documents	Punched tapes
Magazines	Stencils
Magnetic tapes	

Clippings, pamphlets, and small catalogs can be placed in heavy file pockets and filed by subject vertically in correspondence file drawers. Large catalogs, books, and magazines can efficiently be stored on book shelves alphabetically according to the name of the publication. If copies of a magazine are to be kept for more than twelve months, they are sometimes bound or boxed into volumes. Each volume contains copies for one year, and the volumes are stored in chronological order. Phonograph records can be stored like

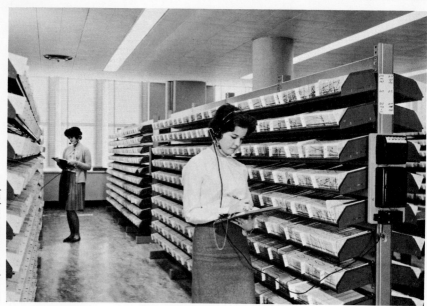

Courtesy Tab Products Company

These file clerks transmit data directly to the customer by telephone.

Courtesy Eastman Kodak Apparatus & Optical Division

Large records can be stored horizontally in these files.

magazines in bound volumes that each contain several phonograph record jackets.

Any large records that are not bulky, such as blueprints, drawings, photographs, maps, certificates and licenses, legal documents, or financial statements, can be stored horizontally in the flat drawers of a file, as illustrated above. Such records frequently are filed numerically, although a subject, an alphabetic, or a geographic arrangement might be satisfactory in some offices. Very large blueprints and drawings are often stored vertically, hanging from hooks in large blueprint cabinets. Mimeograph stencil files that have clips and hangers for vertical storage are also available.

Printing cuts are made of heavy metal but must be protected from damage, especially on the top surface. For this reason they are usually stored face up in shallow, reinforced flat drawers. Bulky items such as motion picture films and magnetic tape reels are usually stored vertically by subject in open wire racks. Large quantities of these items are most efficiently organized numerically. Microfilms are stored in special microfilm files, which will be discussed in Chapter 10. Filmstrips are usually placed in small metal cylinders and stored in flat drawers. The top of each cylinder is labeled for identification. Punched paper tapes can be stored in a variety of ways.

Questions and Problems

1. What advantages do cards have over lists for the organization of information?
2. What are the two types of card files?

3. What is the difference between an index card record and a posted card record?
4. Compare vertical correspondence filing with vertical card filing.
5. What are the standard sizes of file cards?
6. How many guides are needed in a vertical card file?
7. Why are visible files so named?
8. What are signals and for what are they used?
9. Name some types of visible files.
10. Discuss the purpose of a credit system.
11. Discuss the purpose of a purchases and accounts payable system.
12. Discuss the purpose of a shipping and receiving system.
13. Discuss the purpose of a production control system.
14. Discuss the purposes of a payroll system.
15. Discuss the purpose of a cash system.
16. Discuss the purpose of a sales and accounts receivable system.
17. Discuss the purpose of an inventory system.
18. How can the following be filed:
    a. Clippings, pamphlets, and small catalogs?
    b. Large catalogs, books, and magazines?
    c. Phonograph records?
    d. Blueprints, maps, and similar records?
    e. Motion picture films, filmstrips, magnetic tape, and punched paper tape?

Case Problems in Records Management

1. Dexter Associates buys approximately 5,000 cards a month for use in its records system. Wear and tear requires that these cards be replaced four times in the life of the records. The new files supervisor has suggested the use of a more expensive card. She states that in her previous place of employment, for a similar type of record, this better-quality card required replacement only three times in the same period of use. Should the office manager adopt her recommendation? Why?
2. The Mercy Hospital uses a card index at its reception desk to supply information about the room location of its patients. Which do you think would be better for this purpose, a vertical or a visible system? Why?
3. The Apex Electric Motor Company uses a card system for its parts inventory records in the factory stockroom. Which do you think would be better for this purpose, a vertical or a visible system? Why?
4. Select one of the business systems named in this chapter, and make a study of the system in a business firm in your community. Draw up a chart of the source, intermediate, and action records that are used in the business. Compare your chart with the one in this chapter. Describe where and how the records are stored in the business.

5 Alphabetic Filing

MOST OFFICES file correspondence alphabetically according to the name of the writer (for incoming correspondence) or of the addressee (for outgoing correspondence). Alphabetic correspondence filing is popular for three main reasons: it is based on a sequence with which everyone is familiar—the alphabet; it is direct—that is, records can be filed immediately without consulting other files first to secure information; and it is flexible for small or large filing systems—any number of divisions can be created.

Organization

Alphabetic correspondence files vary from small homemade systems requiring only one file drawer to large ready-made (commercial) systems requiring a hundred or more file cabinets. Regardless of the particular system, all alphabetic correspondence files are organized in basically the same way, and most of them have these common elements: (1) primary guides, (2) special guides, also known as secondary or auxiliary guides, (3) individual folders, and (4) miscellaneous folders. Each of these elements will be discussed separately.

1. **Primary Guides.** Primary guides are those that divide the file into major alphabetic sections. These guides are at the beginning of sections. If a file is small it might be divided into only 25 alphabetic sections, the first being A. The A primary guide tells the file worker that all the records behind it,

up to the *B* primary guide, concern those correspondents whose names begin with *A*. The tabs for these primary guides are usually at the extreme left. In very small systems, the primary guide tabs may be staggered from left to right, the arrangement you learned about in Chapter 3.

In general, each primary guide should have at least five and not more than ten folders behind it. Files become cumbersome and expensive to maintain when there are fewer than five folders behind each guide. When there are too many folders behind one guide, the advantages of rapid location and proper support of folders are lost.

2. Special Guides. In many well-organized filing systems, special guides are used after a primary guide to subdivide that section, to highlight important names, or to do both.

3. Individual Folders. Individual folders are arranged alphabetically after each guide. For example, in the following illustration, immediately behind

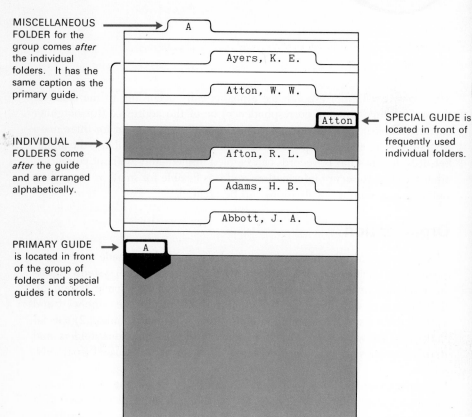

MISCELLANEOUS FOLDER for the group comes *after* the individual folders. It has the same caption as the primary guide.

A

Ayers, K. E.

Atton, W. W.

Atton

SPECIAL GUIDE is located in front of frequently used individual folders.

INDIVIDUAL FOLDERS come *after* the guide and are arranged alphabetically.

Afton, R. L.

Adams, H. B.

Abbott, J. A.

PRIMARY GUIDE is located in front of the group of folders and special guides it controls.

A

The Elements of a Typical Alphabetic Correspondence File

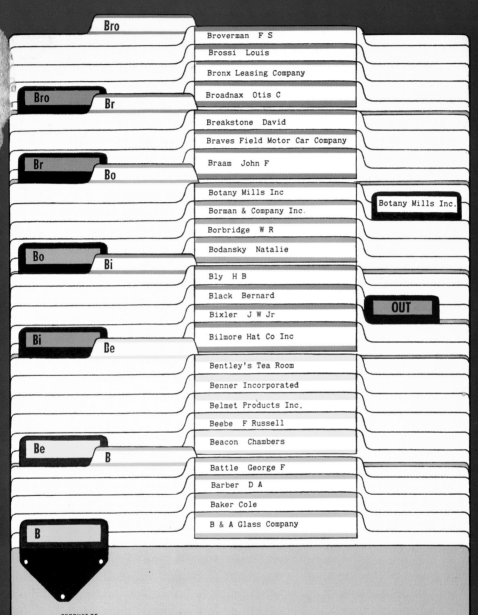

Bro

Broverman F S

Brossi Louis

Bronx Leasing Company

Broadnax Otis C

Bro

Br

Breakstone David

Braves Field Motor Car Company

Br

Braam John F

Bo

Botany Mills Inc

Borman & Company Inc.

Botany Mills Inc.

Borbridge W R

Bo

Bodansky Natalie

Bi

Bly H B

Black Bernard

OUT

Bixler J W Jr

Bi

Bilmore Hat Co Inc

Be

Bentley's Tea Room

Benner Incorporated

Belmet Products Inc.

Beebe F Russell

Be

Beacon Chambers

B

Battle George F

Barber D A

Baker Cole

B

B & A Glass Company

PRODUCT OF
Remington Rand
MADE IN U.S.A.

'LIBRARY BUREAU DEPARTMENT
BRANCHES EVERYWHERE

VARIADEX®
U. S. PATENT NO. 1929383
ARMORCLAD®
GUIDES AND FOLDERS
IN ORDERING GIVE CATALOG
NO. 602—ALSO NUMBER
OF DIVISIONS

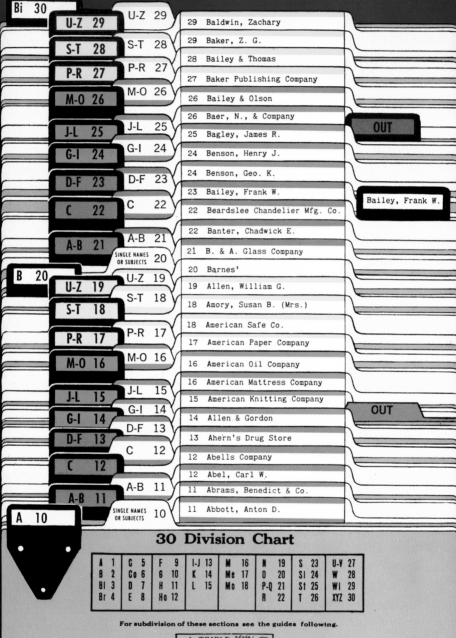

Bi	30				
U-Z	29	U-Z	29	29	Baldwin, Zachary
S-T	28	S-T	28	29	Baker, Z. G.
P-R	27	P-R	27	28	Bailey & Thomas
M-O	26	M-O	26	27	Baker Publishing Company
				26	Bailey & Olson
				26	Baer, N., & Company
J-L	25	J-L	25	25	Bagley, James R.
G-I	24	G-I	24	24	Benson, Henry J.
D-F	23	D-F	23	24	Benson, Geo. K.
				23	Bailey, Frank W.
C	22	C	22	22	Beardslee Chandelier Mfg. Co.
A-B	21	A-B	21	22	Banter, Chadwick E.
		SINGLE NAMES OR SUBJECTS	20	21	B. & A. Glass Company
B	20			20	Barnes'
U-Z	19	U-Z	19	19	Allen, William G.
S-T	18	S-T	18	18	Amory, Susan B. (Mrs.)
				18	American Safe Co.
P-R	17	P-R	17	17	American Paper Company
M-O	16	M-O	16	16	American Oil Company
				16	American Mattress Company
J-L	15	J-L	15	15	American Knitting Company
G-I	14	G-I	14	14	Allen & Gordon
D-F	13	D-F	13	13	Ahern's Drug Store
		C	12	12	Abells Company
C	12			12	Abel, Carl W.
		A-B	11	11	Abrams, Benedict & Co.
A-B	11				
A	10	SINGLE NAMES OR SUBJECTS	10	11	Abbott, Anton D.

OUT

Bailey, Frank W.

OUT

30 Division Chart

A	1	C	5	F	9	I-J	13	M	16	N	19	S	23	U-V	27
B	2	Co	6	G	10	K	14	Me	17	O	20	Si	24	W	28
Bl	3	D	7	H	11	L	15	Mo	18	P-Q	21	St	25	Wi	29
Br	4	E	8	Ho	12					R	22	T	26	XYZ	30

For subdivision of these sections see the guides following.

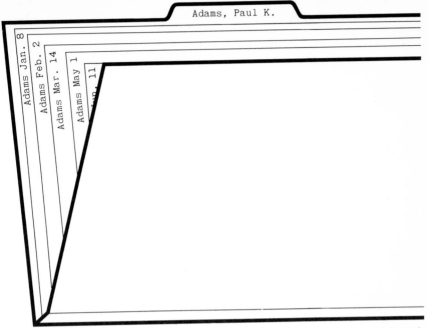

Correspondence in an individual folder is arranged by date, with the record bearing the most recent date in front.

the *A* guide are individual folders for correspondents whose names begin with A. Usually individual folders are not prepared until more than five records relating to a particular correspondent or subject have been received. In an alphabetic correspondence file, you will recognize the individual folders quickly because their tabs contain the full names of correspondents and because the tabs are usually wider than those on guides and on miscellaneous folders. The position of the tabs on individual folders is ordinarily at the center or to the right of center. The records within individual folders are arranged chronologically, as illustrated above, with the latest date in front so that recent correspondence will be easy to locate.

4. Miscellaneous Folders. At the end of every group of individual folders is a *miscellaneous folder*. Note the illustration on page 74. The miscellaneous folder bears the caption *A*, and is for correspondents whose records are filed under *A* but who do not yet warrant an individual folder. Records are usually stored in a miscellaneous folder until five that pertain to a particular correspondent or subject have been accumulated. Both the size of the tab and the caption on a miscellaneous folder correspond to those of the previous primary guide. Miscellaneous folder tabs usually have a position to the left of the individual folder tabs. The records within miscellaneous

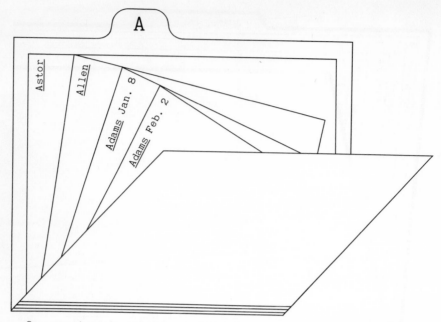

Correspondence in miscellaneous folders is arranged alphabetically. Two or more records for a single correspondent are arranged by date, with the record bearing the most recent date in front.

folders are arranged alphabetically according to the name of the correspondent. If there is more than one record for a correspondent in a miscellaneous folder, his records are arranged chronologically, like those within individual folders.

Alphabetic Storing Procedure

Guides and folders in alphabetic correspondence files are arranged so that if the records have been properly sorted, they can be placed in the folders quickly and efficiently. The steps in the alphabetic correspondence storing procedure are as follows:

1. **Preparation.** The sorted records are taken to the proper file drawer, the label on the drawer is cross-checked with the sorted records, and the drawer is opened. If a file shelf is being used, it is attached to the side or to the front of the drawer and the records are placed on the shelf.

2. **Location of Guide.** The proper guide is selected and pulled forward. For example, if the first record is to be filed in the A section, the A guide is pulled forward.

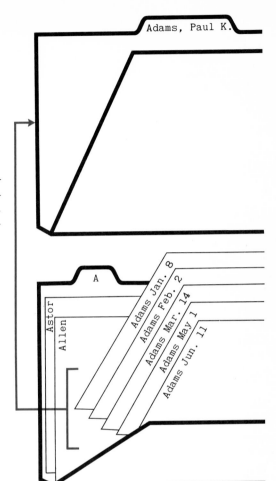

When five or more records for a correspondent have accumulated in a miscellaneous folder, an individual folder is prepared.

3. Location of Individual Folder. The tabs of the individual folders behind the guide are scanned. If there is an individual folder for the record, the record is placed inside the folder.

4. Location of Miscellaneous Folder. If there is no individual folder for the record, all of the individual folders in the section are pulled forward, exposing the miscellaneous folder for the section. The record is then placed inside the miscellaneous folder. (If the miscellaneous folder had been in front of the individual folders instead of behind them, the file worker would have had to reverse the direction of his work—a waste of time—after discovering that there was no individual folder for the record.)

Within miscellaneous folders, related papers can be stapled together for convenience in removing them from folders and for keeping them in their proper order. Paper clips should not be used for fastening together filed papers because they are excessively bulky, tend to catch on adjacent sheets of paper, and slip off the papers during the filing and finding process. Paper clips should be used only as temporary fasteners for desk work—they have no place in the files.

Alphabetic Filing Systems

Guides, folders, and other materials for an alphabetic correspondence filing system may be purchased separately or as complete units. When they are bought separately and the system is organized by the office workers themselves, the system is called an *office-planned alphabetic system* (homemade system). When the system is sold commercially as a unit—guides, folders, and other materials—the system is called a *commercial alphabetic system* (ready-made system). Either type of system can provide for from 25 to 200,000 or more primary divisions of the alphabet.

Office-Planned Alphabetic Systems. Many offices, because they have special needs or simply because they desire to set up their own filing system, purchase guides and folders in sufficient quantity to make an alphabetic filing system. The guides have tabs with inserts for the captions; and folder labels, both individual and miscellaneous, are prepared in the office. An office-planned alphabetic system is advantageous when the office manager or other person in charge of the records knows exactly what arrangement of guides and folders is best for the filing procedures of that office. But office-planned alphabetic systems sometimes are unsatisfactory because they are oversimplified and do not provide the efficiencies in filing and finding that are available in commercial alphabetic systems. Because many businesses have difficulty in organizing their own filing systems, they often request help from records management experts, who can study a firm's needs and work out the most satisfactory system.

Commercial Alphabetic Systems. Most large file-supply companies manufacture patented filing systems that are complete except for the captions on individual folders. There are many kinds of commercial systems designed for a broad range of business requirements, and businesses use these systems because they have special features that speed up filing work. Such features include: (1) the use of color as a double check against misfiling, (2) numeric captions combined with the alphabetic captions for a filing double check, and (3) the use of special guides to highlight important names or to subdivide major alphabetic sections. To illustrate some of the special features and variations in guide and folder characteristics, a few commercial alphabetic systems are described on the following pages. Color illustrations of the first two systems described will be found opposite pages 72 and 73.

Variadex System
(manufactured by Remington Rand Division, Sperry Rand Corporation)

PRIMARY GUIDES	SPECIAL GUIDES	INDIVIDUAL FOLDERS	MISC. FOLDERS
Single captions, tab in first position.	Used for names having a large volume of correspondence. Tab in fourth position.	Tab in third position.	Tab in second position. Folder is behind the group of individual folders.

Special Features. Guide and folder tabs of various colors help to speed up the location of records and help to prevent misfiling. The colors of the primary guide tabs appear in rainbow sequence, and the folder tabs are of the same color as the primary guide before them. Hence a file worker would know that he was misfiling if he placed a folder with a yellow tab among folders with green tabs. The following chart indicates how the various colors are assigned to the guides and folders.

IF THE SECOND LETTER OF THE FIRST UNIT OF THE NAME IS:	AS IN:	THE COLOR ON THE GUIDE AND FOLDER TABS FOR THAT SECTION WILL BE:
a,b,c,d (or no second letter)	Baker	orange
e,f,g, or h	Bennett	yellow
i,j,k,l,m, or n	Binney	green
o,p, or q	Bond	blue
r,s,t,u,v,w,x,y, or z	Brattle	violet

As the chart indicates, a name in which the first unit has no second letter, as in the *A and B Company,* is filed under orange. The *second* letter of the first unit is used to separate the color sections because 78 percent of second letters are vowels, and these vowels conveniently divide the alphabet into equal sections. In addition, using the first, rather than the second, letter of the first unit would create large sections of the files with the same color and much of the advantage of using color would be lost.

In the Variadex system, then, the name *Robert Abbott* is filed under orange, because *Abbott* is the first unit and *b* is the second letter of that first unit.

The name *Turner Construction Company* is filed under violet, because *Turner* is the first unit and *u* is the second letter of that first unit.

Triple-Check Automatic Index
(manufactured by Remington Rand Division, Sperry Rand Corporation)

PRIMARY GUIDES	SPECIAL GUIDES	INDIVIDUAL FOLDERS	MISC. FOLDERS
Single captions, tab in first position.	Two kinds: alphabetic subdivision guides (second position) and common name or subject guides (fifth position).	Tab in fourth position.	Tab in third position. Folder is behind the group of individual folders. Same caption as the previous special guide.

Special Features. Section numbers are used to increase speed and accuracy. A uniform set of nine special alphabetic subdivision guides follows each primary guide. The primary guides are numbered according to a primary number chart, shown in the illustration opposite page 73. This chart would be used when there are 30 primary guides in the set purchased. If more primary guides are used, another numbering chart would be used to correspond with the increased number of primary guides. The special alphabetic subdivisions are also numbered. Since there are always nine alphabetic subdivisions behind each primary guide, they are always numbered the same, from 1–9, according to the following divisions of the alphabet: *A–B*, 1; *C*, 2; *D–F*, 3; *G–I*, 4; *J–L*, 5; *M–O*, 6; *P–R*, 7; *S–T*, 8; *U–Z*, 9. These subdivision numbers are always preceded by all except the last digit of the code number for the preceding primary guide. Thus, if the primary guide for *B* has the code number 20, the code number of the first subdivision guide is 21, the second 22, and so on.

The illustration for the 30-division chart lists the code numbers for the primary guides, except that the last digit, which is always zero, is omitted. On the chart, then, the code number for *A* is listed as 1, but the *A* primary guide caption would be 10; *Bi* is listed as 3, but the *Bi* guide would bear the number 30.

The primary guides are used exactly the same as the alphabetic guides in any alphabetic system of filing—to locate the *first* units of the name. The special alphabetic guides, however, are used to subdivide records filed after the primary guide according to the *second* unit of the name. As in all systems using section numbers, correspondence filed in a Triple-Check file is coded by writing the code number on the piece of correspondence in addition to writing or underlining the name under which it is to be filed. The following chart indicates how three names are coded in the Triple-Check Automatic Index:

NAME BY UNITS			PRIMARY CODE	SUBDIVISION CODE	FILED BEHIND PRIMARY GUIDE:	FILED BEHIND SUBDIVISION GUIDE:	FILED IN FOLDER:
1	2	3					
Abel	Carl	W.	10 (*A*bel)	2 (*C*arl)	10	12	12, Abel, Carl W. *or* C-12 (misc.)
Fox	Book Co.		90 (*F*ox)	1 (*B*ook)	90	91	91, Fox Book Co. *or* B-91 (misc.)
Barnes'			20 (*B*arnes')	0 (no second unit)	20	None	20, Barnes' *or* "Single Names or Subjects" (misc.)

Correspondence to be filed under the three names above would be coded according to the number of their respective subdivision guides. Since there are no subdivision guides for single names or subjects, *Barnes'* would be coded according to its primary guide, 20.

Color is also used to help the file worker identify guide and folder tabs. The tabs of the first three alphabetic subdivision guides in each section are tan, the next three are green, and the last three are yellow. The colors of the labels on the individual folders and on the miscellaneous folders match the special subdivision guides they follow. Primary guide and single-name or subject folder tabs are white.

Colorscan
(*manufactured by Remington Rand Division, Sperry Rand Corporation*)

PRIMARY GUIDES	*SPECIAL GUIDES*	*INDIVIDUAL FOLDERS*	*MISC. FOLDERS*
Single captions, tabs are white and are located in first position.	Called *action guides*, tabs are in second position.	Entire folder is a distinctive color, depending upon first letter of second unit. Tabs in third position.	Tabs in fourth position.

Special Features. Color-coded *action guides* are positioned to the right of the primary guide and systematically precede each color break for second units on the individual folders. The entire folder is colored according to the following chart, which is continued on page 80.

FIRST LETTER OF SECOND UNIT	*COLOR OF FOLDER*
A–B	Red
C	Yellow
D–E–F	Pink
G–H–I	Green

FIRST LETTER OF SECOND UNIT	COLOR OF FOLDER
J–K–L	Brown
M–N–O	Blue
P–Q–R	Orange
S–T	Purple
U–V–W–X–Y–Z	Gold

To return an individual folder, *simply place it at the front of its color section*. Active folders remain in the front through frequency of use, and less active folders move to the rear. This is an example of random filing, which works for most operations because 80 percent of the file activity takes place in only 20 percent of the files. Single-name folders (no second unit), such as Rubbermaid, are white and are filed immediately behind the primary guide.

Amberg Nual Alphabet Index
(manufactured by Amberg File & Index Company)

PRIMARY GUIDES	SPECIAL GUIDES	INDIVIDUAL FOLDERS	MISC. FOLDERS
Double captions, tabs staggered in second, third, and fourth positions.	Called "leader equipment" in this system. Tabs in first position.	Tabs staggered in approximately the second, third, and fourth positions.	Tab in first position. Folder is in *front* of the individual folders.

Special Features. Section numbers are used to speed up filing and finding and to safeguard against misfiling. The primary guides are numbered consecutively. All special guides, individual folders, and the miscellaneous folder bear the same number as the primary guide they follow.

F. E. Bee Line Filing System
(manufactured by the Filing Equipment Bureau)

PRIMARY GUIDES	SPECIAL GUIDES	INDIVIDUAL FOLDERS	MISC. FOLDERS
Single captions, tabs in first position.	Tabs in fourth position.	Tabs in third position.	Tab in second position. Folder is behind the individual folders.

Special Features. Section numbers are used to speed up filing and finding and to safeguard against misfiling. The primary guides are numbered consecutively. All special guides, individual folders, and the miscellaneous folder bear the same number as the primary guide they follow. Color is used to aid in identification—miscellaneous folder tabs are salmon-colored; individual folders are obtainable with tabs of various colors that can be used to distinguish the folders in any manner desired in a particular office.

Safeguard Index

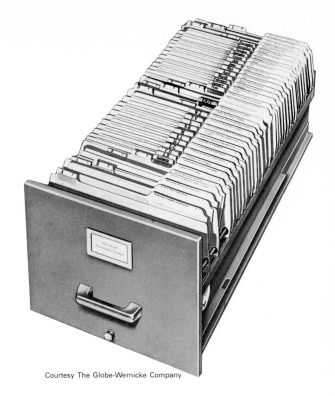

Courtesy The Globe-Wernicke Company

Safeguard Index (*manufactured by Globe-Wernicke*)

PRIMARY GUIDES	SPECIAL GUIDES	INDIVIDUAL FOLDERS	MISC. FOLDERS
Single captions, tabs staggered in first, second, and third positions.	Tabs in fourth position.	Tabs in fifth position.	Tabs in first, second, and third positions. Folder is behind the individual folders.

Special Features. Section numbers are used to increase speed and accuracy. The primary guides are numbered consecutively. All special guides, individual folders, and the miscellaneous folder bear the same number as the primary guide they follow. Color is used to differentiate between guides, miscellaneous folders, and individual folders. All primary guide tabs are green and all miscellaneous folder tabs are red. Labels of various colors can be used to classify individual folder tabs. Because the miscellaneous folder tabs and the primary guide tabs are in the same position, the primary guide tabs are made more conspicuous by standing a little higher than the miscellaneous folder tabs.

Super-Ideal Filing System

Courtesy The Shaw-Walker Company

Super-Ideal System (*manufactured by Shaw-Walker*)

PRIMARY GUIDES	SPECIAL GUIDES	INDIVIDUAL FOLDERS	MISC. FOLDERS
Tabs staggered in first and second position (see below for description of captions).	Tabs in third position.	Tabs staggered in second and third position.	Tabs in first position. Folder is behind the individual folders.

Special Features. Section numbers are used to increase speed and accuracy. The primary guides are numbered consecutively. The special guides, the individual folders, and the miscellaneous folder bear the same number as the primary guide they follow. Special guides are used to highlight important names, and in addition, special folders are used to subdivide the correspondence concerning these important names. This subdivision is based on time periods, and the number of these special folders depends on the volume of records pertaining to the correspondent. Special subguides are used to index the time-period folders when there are six or more. The top edge of all folder tabs is just below the guide captions to increase visibility for the guide captions. Guide captions are of the *multiple type*—they not only indicate the beginning and ending of a section but also the most frequently used parts of a section.

Y and E Direct-Name Index

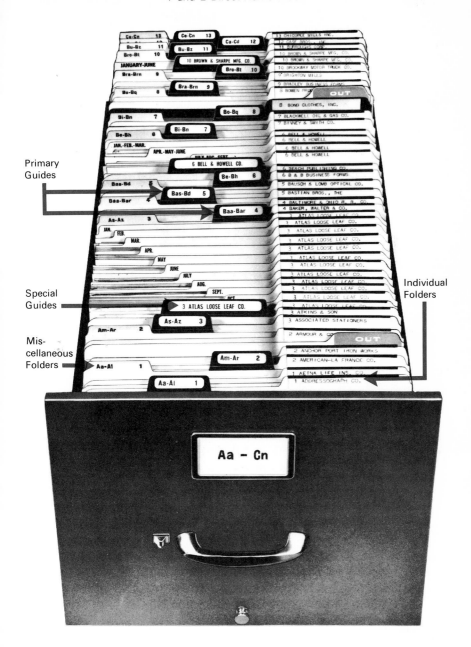

Primary Guides

Special Guides

Miscellaneous Folders

Individual Folders

Y and E Direct-Name Index (*manufactured by Yawman and Erbe*)

PRIMARY GUIDES	SPECIAL GUIDES	INDIVIDUAL FOLDERS	MISC. FOLDERS
Double captions, tabs staggered in the second and third positions.	Double-width tabs in second and third positions.	Tabs in fourth position.	Tabs in first position. Folder is behind the individual folders.

Special Features. Section numbers are used to speed up filing and finding and to safeguard against misfiling. The primary guides are numbered consecutively. The special guides, the individual folders, and the miscellaneous folder bear the same number as the primary guide they follow.

On primary guides in sets of more than 40, each caption beginning with a new letter of the alphabet is printed in red. All other guide captions are printed in black, and the captions on miscellaneous folders are printed in red.

Individual folders can be obtained with extra-wide tabs in two heights for subdividing by time period the records of important correspondents.

Tell-I-Vision System
(*manufactured by Smead Manufacturing Company*)

PRIMARY GUIDES	SPECIAL GUIDES	INDIVIDUAL FOLDERS	MISC. FOLDERS
Single captions, tabs staggered in the first and second positions.	Available to signal more frequently used individual folders.	Wide tabs extend across fourth and fifth positions.	Tabs in third position. Folder is behind the individual folders.

Special Features. An alphabetic color system (blue and orange) guides the eye in finding folders, and a numeric color signal system speeds replacement of folders in the file. The number on the folder tab corresponds to the number on the primary guide of the section in which the folder belongs. Miscellaneous folders with green tabs act as primary transfer file guides as well as folder guides when old files are placed in inactive storage. New miscellaneous and individual folders are prepared to equip the active file for another period. When the system expands, current primary guides remain unchanged. Only new folders and the necessary number of additional guides are added.

Questions and Problems

1. What are the reasons for the popularity of alphabetic correspondence filing?
2. What elements are common to most alphabetic correspondence files?
3. What is a primary guide, and where is it located?
4. When is a special guide used?

5. Where are individual folders located in alphabetic correspondence files? How are the records arranged within such folders?
6. Where are miscellaneous folders located in alphabetic correspondence files? How are the records arranged within these folders?
7. Describe the procedure used in storing records in alphabetic correspondence files.
8. What special features do most commercial systems have that make them more efficient than homemade systems?
9. Variadex System:
   a. What type of caption is on the tabs?
   b. From left to right, what is the arrangement of the guides? of the folders?
   c. From front to back, what is the arrangement of guides and folders?
   d. How is color used?
10. Triple-Check Automatic Index:
    a. What type of caption is on the tabs?
    b. From left to right, what is the arrangement of the guides? of the folders?
    c. From front to back, what is the arrangement of guides and folders?
    d. How are numbers used?
    e. How is color used?
11. Colorscan System:
    a. What type of caption is on the tabs?
    b. From left to right, what is the arrangement of the guides? of the folders?
    c. From front to back, what is the arrangement of guides and folders?
    d. How is color used?
12. Amberg Nual Alphabetic Index:
    a. What type of caption is on the tabs?
    b. From left to right, what is the arrangement of the guides? of the folders?
    c. From front to back, what is the arrangement of guides and folders?
    d. How are numbers used?
13. F. E. Bee Line Filing System:
    a. What type of caption is on the tabs?
    b. From left to right, what is the arrangement of the guides? of the folders?
    c. From front to back, what is the arrangement of guides and folders?
    d. How are numbers used?
    e. How is color used?
14. Safeguard Index:
    a. What type of caption is on the tabs?
    b. What is the arrangement of the guides? of the folders?
    c. From front to back, what is the arrangement of guides and folders?

  d. How are numbers used?

  e. How is color used?

  f. Are the tabs of the folders and guides the same height?

15. Super-Ideal System:

  a. What type of caption is on the tabs?

  b. From left to right, what is the arrangement of the guides?   of the folders?

  c. From front to back, what is the arrangement of guides and folders?

  d. How are numbers used?

  e. How is important correspondence from an individual subdivided?

  f. Are the tabs of the folders and guides the same height?

16. Y and E Direct-Name Index:

  a. What type of caption is on the tabs?

  b. From left to right, what is the arrangement of the guides?   of the folders?

  c. From front to back, what is the arrangement of guides and folders?

  d. How are numbers used?

  e. How is color used?

  f. How are individual folders further subdivided?

17. Tell-I-Vision System:

  a. What type of caption is on the tabs?

  b. From left to right, what is the arrangement of the guides?   of the folders?

  c. From front to back, what is the arrangement of guides and folders?

  d. How are numbers used?

  e. How is color used?

  f. How are the folders used at transfer time?

Case Problems in Records Management

1. Ralph Perkins, who is the only office worker in a small organization, decides not to have miscellaneous folders in the files. As soon as the first record pertaining to any correspondent or subject has to be filed, he intends to prepare an individual folder. Do you approve? Why?

2. Jean Abbott works for a small organization. She thinks it would be a good idea to let at least ten records accumulate in the miscellaneous folders for any one name or subject before preparing an individual folder. What do you think of such a procedure?   Why?

3. Agnes Watkins works in an office where the records filed vary considerably in size and many of them are smaller than standard-size letters. She attributes a recent increase in records loss to this size difference and has suggested that all records within any one folder be fastened to the folder. Do you approve of her suggestion?   Why?

4. An individual folder for the Peter Curtis Company contains records dating back six months. Approximately half of the folder's contents are letters; the other half are an assortment of catalogs and other records. It is now time to prepare a second folder for the Peter Curtis Company because the maximum working capacity of the first one has been reached. How would you divide the records to be placed in each folder and what information would you type on the folder labels?

5. There are 40 individual folders behind the *J* guide in the files of the Paramount Company. Of these, 20 bear captions containing the name *Jones*. File workers complain they are slowed considerably in storing and finding records in the *Jones* folders and in the folders following the *Jones* folders. What would you suggest to alleviate the situation?

6 *Numeric Filing*

NUMERIC FILING is the arrangement of records according to code numbers. The code number may be assigned to the record by the file worker, or it may be a part of the record itself (such as the number that appears on an invoice or a check). When records are filed in consecutive order according to these code numbers, *serial*, or *consecutive*, numeric filing is employed. Other methods of arranging records numerically are discussed later in the chapter.

Alphabetic filing systems are called *direct systems* because a file worker can go directly to the file drawer and, by means of the name captions, find the records for which he is searching. Numeric filing systems, however, are *indirect*; that is, the file worker must first consult an alphabetic index to determine the code number of a record. In a numeric system, for example, if the sales manager says, "I would like to see William Hart's letter of April 17," the file worker refers to an alphabetic card index, or an alphabetic list, which tells him the number under which Mr. Hart's letter is filed. After he finds the number, he goes to the folder on which the number appears and locates the letter from Mr. Hart.

Why Businesses Use Numeric Filing

Even though numeric filing may appear to require double effort, businesses find that it has certain advantages over alphabetic filing: (1) Numeric systems make possible quick sequential identification of records. Therefore, once

A lawyer's files may contain two
numeric folders with correspondence from the same client (J. B.
Adams), but they may concern
separate cases (Bryan and Fox).

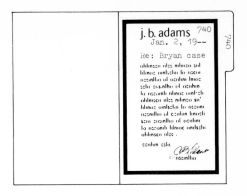

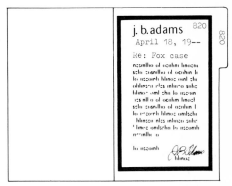

A firm may file forms by order
number.

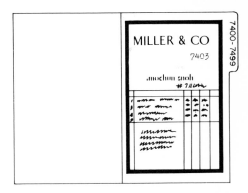

records have been coded numerically, they are easier to file and find than
records coded alphabetically. Also, duplication is avoided through the use
of numbers rather than names. Names can be the same, but folders can always
have different numbers. (2) Numeric systems provide for convenient expansion. The alphabet is limited to 26 letters, but additional numbers can always
be assigned at the end of a numeric file. (3) There is plenty of opportunity for

permanent and extensive cross-referencing. Such systems usually require an alphabetic card index, and this index is useful for cross-referencing. (4) The card index, besides being a reference to the numeric file, is a handy, compact list of all the names and addresses of correspondents and subjects; and it may include various useful facts about them.

Each of the advantages listed here is particularly attractive for the types of business operations discussed below.

1. *Business operations that require accurate, quick, and positive identification of records.* If the names on orders can be positively identified by a number, it is more likely that the proper person or company will receive and be charged for a shipment of merchandise and that his account will be properly credited when payment is made. (This is because orders are usually filled by numbers rather than by the names of customers.) Accounting departments often file vouchers by their numbers; insurance companies generally use policy numbers rather than policyholders' names; and in confidential situations records are often filed numerically to conceal the names of the people or organizations involved.

2. *Business operations in which the files are rapidly expanding.* In businesses with growing numbers of files, numeric filing can be used to avoid juggling files. For example, once an alphabetic file has reached its capacity, there are two methods of expansion. Another alphabetic file may be set up in new cabinets; but two sets of cabinets, each containing its own alphabetic files, are cumbersome to operate. Or the present records may be shifted so they will be evenly distributed in a larger number of cabinets (a time-consuming operation). But numeric filing avoids both of these inefficient methods. Once the numeric file has reached its capacity, new numbers and new cabinets may be added at the *end* of the present file; juggling is unnecessary.

3. *Business operations that require permanent and extensive cross-referencing.* Some businesses, such as law firms and contractors, deal with records that refer to definite cases, contracts, or operations that are active for relatively long and indefinite periods. Because each case, contract, or operation usually refers to several names or several other cases, an extensive cross-reference is necessary. This can be provided in the card index of a numeric file. To illustrate, a lawyer might represent the same client in several cases. In the card index one card bearing the client's name would refer to each of the cases by number. The records concerning each separate case would be filed in separately numbered folders. Thus, all of the cross-referencing for a client is done on the same card, and the numeric file is uncluttered by numerous cross-reference sheets.

4. *Business operations where a card index is desirable.* Many mail-order businesses use the card index of a numeric file as a mailing list. A card index can also be used to record such facts as credit ratings of customers, products of suppliers, and salaries of employees.

Organization of a Numeric Correspondence File

A numeric correspondence file system has three major parts, as illustrated below. They are (1) the main numeric file, (2) the miscellaneous alphabetic file, and (3) the card index.

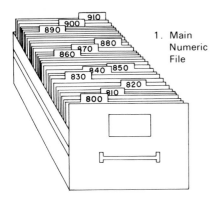

1. Main Numeric File

The Three Elements of a Numeric Correspondence Filing System

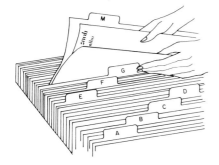

2. Miscellaneous Alphabetic File

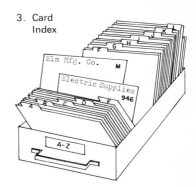

3. Card Index

The Main Numeric File. The main numeric file contains guides and individual folders that bear numeric captions. Each folder contains records concerning a separate correspondent. As in alphabetic filing, the records within the folders are arranged chronologically with the record bearing the latest date in front. There is a numeric guide for each group of five to ten folders. Because folders are arranged in sequence behind guides and are easy to locate, they often have no tabs, in which case folder numbers are printed in the upper right corner on either the front or the back flap of the folder.

As a new correspondent or subject develops and when an individual folder is warranted, a number is assigned. Prenumbered, unused folders are often stored in the last drawer of the file. The next unused number is assigned to the new correspondent. Sometimes a register similar to the one illustrated

A Numeric File Register

NO.	NAME	DATE
800	Hancock, Phillip E.	6/12/--
801	Avco Inc.	6/12/--
802	Young and Stephens Co.	6/13/--
803	G - W Builders Supply	6/15/--
804	Noland Wholesale Inc.	6/15/--
805	Bullock, J. D., Jr.	6/16/--
806	Louise's Shop	6/16/--
807	Johnson-Whitney Furn. Co.	6/16/--
808		
809		
810		

above is kept. This register shows the names and numbers already assigned and the numbers available. Therefore, there is never a question as to what number to assign, and this number is the correspondent's until there are no longer any records relative to him in the files. At that time, the number may be reassigned.

Numeric guides may be arranged in several ways. In the illustration on page 91, the numeric guide tabs are in three positions, staggered from left to right. There are two other convenient arrangements of guides and folders in the main numeric file: (1) The guide tabs may appear in two (or three) positions on the left, and the folder tabs (if any), in the last position on the right. (2) The guide tabs may appear in the center only, and the folder tabs, in two positions to the left and two positions to the right of the center. Guide tabs are numbered in fives or tens, or for systems in which one folder contains ten numbers, in hundreds.

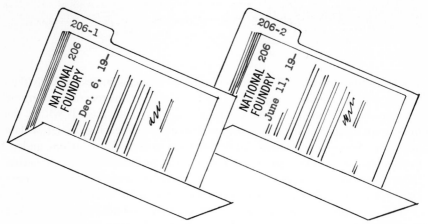

To prevent overcrowding, these numeric folders have been subdivided by date. The correspondence bearing the most recent date is stored in the front folder, or 206-1.

When a numeric folder becomes full, the records can be subdivided by date or subject, depending on how they will be requested. When the records are subdivided and half of them are placed in a new folder, both the new and the old folder bear the same caption as the old one, plus an auxiliary number. The auxiliary number gives further identification—for example, Folder 206 upon being subdivided becomes 206-2 and the new folder is 206-1. This is illustrated on page 92.

The Miscellaneous Alphabetic File. The miscellaneous alphabetic file contains guides and folders bearing alphabetic captions. Its purpose is to provide a place to store pieces of correspondence that do not warrant individual folders in the main numeric file. Therefore, every folder in this file is a miscellaneous folder containing the records of several correspondents. Records, of course, proceed in strict alphabetic order throughout the file. When five or more records concerning one correspondent accumulate, they are assigned the next unused number, are placed in a numeric folder corresponding to this number, and are stored in the main numeric file.

The miscellaneous alphabetic file can be in the front of the first drawer of the main numeric file, in a separate drawer of the main numeric file, or in a separate filing cabinet.

The Card Index. The card index, arranged alphabetically, contains cards, each with the name (and usually the address and other information) of a correspondent, together with the code number assigned to his records. This type of index is necessary in all numeric correspondence systems because correspondence is nearly always called for by name rather than by number. If the records are kept in the miscellaneous alphabetic file, this is indicated on the card by the symbol *M*. The *M* is eliminated and a folder number is written in its place when the correspondent is assigned a folder in the main numeric file.

Cross-Referencing

You will recall that cross-referencing in alphabetic systems is accomplished by placing cross-reference sheets or photocopies of the original document in the individual and miscellaneous folders. In numeric systems, however, cross-referencing is usually done in the card index on cross-reference cards. The card illustrated on page 95 would be filed under *C* in the card index. If a file worker were asked for information concerning the Carter Bread Company, the name of which has been changed to Homemade Bakeries, he would find the Carter Bread Company card and see that the records are filed in the folder for Homemade Bakeries under the numeric caption 248.

How Correspondence Is Coded and Stored in a Numeric System

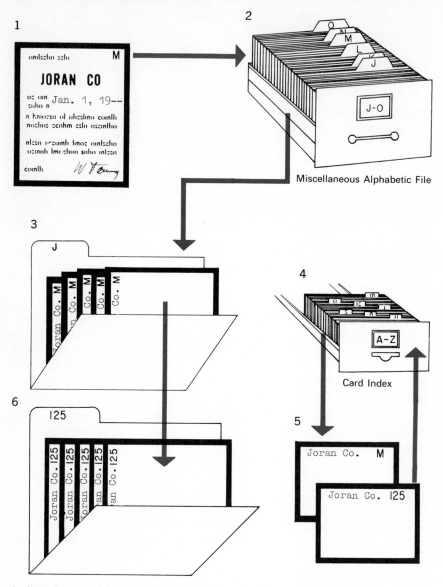

An incoming record from a new correspondent (1) is coded "M" and stored in the miscellaneous alphabetic file (2). As soon as five records concerning this correspondent accumulate (3), the card index (4) is consulted. The next unassigned number (5) is given to this correspondent, and the notation on the card is changed from "M" to "125." The records are then recoded "125" and transferred to a numeric folder (6), which is stored in the main numeric file.

Steps in Numeric Filing

The steps in numeric filing are illustrated on page 96.

Steps 1, 2, and 3 are explained fully in the illustration. In Step 4, in numeric coding if the card index shows that no number has been assigned to a correspondent or subject, an *M* is placed in the upper right corner to indicate that the record is to be stored in the miscellaneous alphabetic file. If there is no card in the index for the correspondent, the file worker should prepare the card and place it in the index before he stores the correspondence in the miscellaneous alphabetic file. In performing numeric coding, the file worker should remember that code numbers are easily misread, and he should be extremely careful in writing them. To keep file workers from confusing with code numbers any other numbers that may be written on correspondence, colored pencils are often used for coding.

In Step 5, numeric sorting, the records are arranged first by hundreds, then by tens, and finally by correct numeric sequence within these divisions. Correspondence coded *M* is separated from the numerically coded correspondence and sorted alphabetically during this step.

In Step 6, storing, correspondence coded *M* is stored in the proper folders in the miscellaneous alphabetic file and numerically coded correspondence is stored in the main numeric file. Great care must be taken when records are stored according to code numbers because when numbers are read hurriedly, the digits are often transposed. For example, the number 4532 may be hurriedly read as 4352. This kind of error is not as obvious as misspelling the name *Jones* as *Joens*. Because numeric errors are harder to detect than errors in names, accuracy is extremely important for anyone doing either the coding or the storing in a numeric system. Some businesses periodically check the accuracy of their numeric files to ensure that the records have been coded correctly and stored in the proper folders.

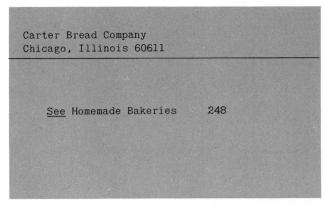

```
Carter Bread Company
Chicago, Illinois 60611



     See Homemade Bakeries      248
```

A Cross-Reference in the Card Index to the Main Numeric File

Steps in the Numeric Filing of Correspondence

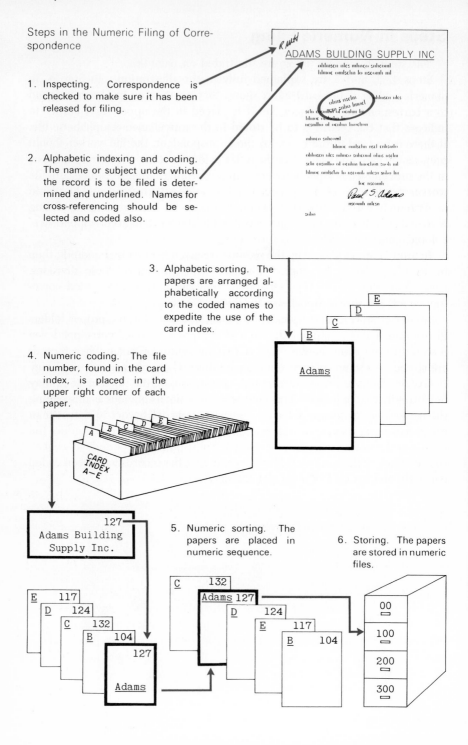

1. Inspecting. Correspondence is checked to make sure it has been released for filing.

2. Alphabetic indexing and coding. The name or subject under which the record is to be filed is determined and underlined. Names for cross-referencing should be selected and coded also.

3. Alphabetic sorting. The papers are arranged alphabetically according to the coded names to expedite the use of the card index.

4. Numeric coding. The file number, found in the card index, is placed in the upper right corner of each paper.

5. Numeric sorting. The papers are placed in numeric sequence.

6. Storing. The papers are stored in numeric files.

Other Numeric Systems

There are other numeric systems used in business besides the consecutive, or serial, type, which has been discussed previously. Among these systems are (1) terminal-digit systems, (2) triple-digit systems, (3) middle-digit systems, and (4) duplex-numeric systems.

In *terminal-digit* systems the numbers are read from right to left. The numbers are generally analyzed in three parts. The last, or terminal, two digits are the drawer number, the next two digits are the folder number, and all other digits indicate the sequence in the folder. To illustrate, an insurance policy numbered 421597 would be stored in the drawer numbered 97 (last two digits) and in the folder numbered 15 (middle two digits), and the 42 (first two digits) would determine its sequence in the folder. Terminal-digit systems have the advantages of an even distribution of records in the files at all times and permanent numbering of cabinets and primary guides, even after records have been transferred. The illustration on page 98 compares consecutive-number and terminal-digit systems.

Triple-digit systems are similar to terminal-digit systems except that the numbers are broken into two parts, instead of three. The last three digits of a number on the extreme right are called *primary numbers*, and the remaining digits determine the sequence of records in the folder bearing the primary numbers. For example, Insurance Policy No. 421597 would be stored in Folder 597. The 421 would determine its sequence in the folder.

In *middle-digit* systems (sometimes called *significant-number systems*), records are separated first according to the third and fourth digits from the right of a number, then according to the first two digits on the left, and finally according to the last two digits on the right. For example, Insurance Policy No. 421597 would be stored in Drawer 15 (middle two digits), and in Folder 42 (first two digits). The 97 would determine its sequence in the folder.

Duplex-numeric systems use digits and letters of the alphabet, separated by hyphens or commas, to code records numerically. In Chapter 7 there is a further discussion of this system.

Numeric Card Files

Numeric filing is frequently used for card records. For example, accounts receivable ledger cards might be filed by customer account number, inventory cards by part number, employee earnings record cards by employee number, and accounts payable ledger cards by vendor number. Just as with correspondence, either serial, terminal-digit, triple-digit, middle-digit, or duplex-numeric sequencing may be used for cards filed numerically. Punched cards used in data processing are very frequently kept in numeric sequence because punched cards can be sequenced faster numerically than alphabetically on data processing machines.

A Comparison of Consecutive Number and Terminal-Digit Systems

If many forms have to be filed by several file workers, the terminal-digit system is advantageous because it overcomes crowded working conditions by spreading the work over several file drawers.

If you were filing business forms bearing these numbers:

23753
23747
23750
23752
23756
23755

1. In a consecutive number system

2. In a terminal digit system

A. The numbers would be broken into these sets.

Sequence in folder	Folder number	Drawer number
2	37	47
2	37	50
2	37	52
2	37	53
2	37	55
2	37	56

B. Reading the numbers from right to left, you would file forms first by drawer number, and finally by sequence in folder.

Thus the six forms would be stored in six separate file drawers (starred). They would each be stored in folder 37 in their respective drawers.

They would all be filed in numeric order in one drawer (starred).

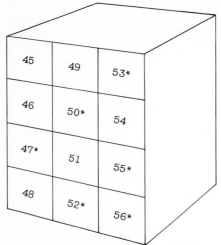

The basic principles of numeric card filing are similar to those for numeric correspondence filing. One difference, of course, is that the cards are filed independently behind numeric guides rather than in file folders. However, if numerically filed cards refer to individual or company names or to items of merchandise, it is necessary that an alphabetic list of these names or items, together with the numbers assigned to them, be kept as part of the numeric card system. This list, or index, is used to locate names or items when the number is not known. Numeric filing as it relates to subject filing is discussed in the next chapter.

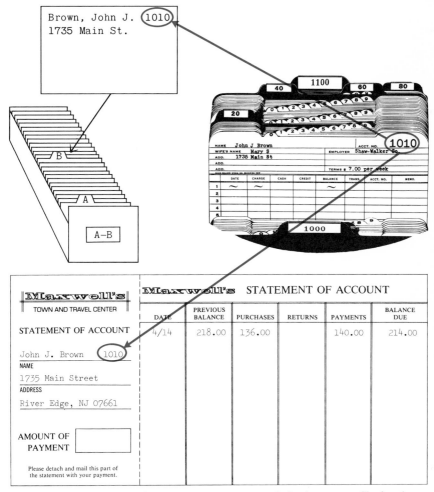

This numeric card file for customer account cards is the source file for the preparation of the monthly statement shown at the bottom. The card file at the upper left is an alphabetic index to customer account numbers.

Questions and Problems

1. What is numeric filing?
2. What is meant by direct and indirect filing systems?
3. Describe types of business operations in which numeric filing systems can be used to advantage.
4. What are the three parts of a numeric system?
5. Are there any miscellaneous folders in the main numeric file?
6. How are the records arranged within the individual folders?
7. When is a number assigned to a correspondent or a subject? How long does it keep this number?
8. Where is the number printed on the folder?
9. How are guides and folders arranged in the main numeric file?
10. What is done when a numbered folder is filled to capacity?
11. Why is a miscellaneous alphabetic file needed in a numeric system?
12. Where is the miscellaneous alphabetic file of a numeric system kept?
13. What is the purpose of a register in a numeric system?
14. Why is a card index needed in numeric filing?
15. What information would usually be recorded on each card in the card index of a numeric system?
16. What does the symbol *M* on a card in the card index mean?
17. How are cards arranged in the index to a numeric file?
18. Compare cross-referencing in alphabetic and numeric systems.
19. Enumerate and describe the steps in numeric filing.
20. What is a common cause of error in numeric filing? What safeguard can be adopted?
21. Describe how numbers are used for filing in terminal-digit, triple-digit, and middle-digit systems.
22. What are the advantages of the terminal-digit, triple-digit, and middle-digit systems over the serial, or consecutive, numeric systems?
23. Discuss the similarities and differences between numeric correspondence filing and numeric card filing.

Case Problems in Records Management

1. The John P. Vanderbilt Company uses a numeric filing system. Because of the nature of their operations, the individual folders most recently assigned are used most frequently. As a result, the four file workers are quite often working in the same area. What would you suggest to eliminate the congestion?
2. Ellen Barton, a file worker, asks her supervisor why their company does not change from numeric filing to some other system because of these disadvantages:

a. Records cannot be stored directly in the files because reference has to be made first to the card index to determine folder numbers.

b. Upon their receipt, records must be coded twice.

c. Time is lost on cross-referenced records because the numbered folder listed in the card index for the correspondent refers the file worker to another folder.

Assuming that a numeric system is best for the company's needs, can any of Miss Barton's objections be eliminated?

3. Every deliveryman for the National Milk Company has a loose-leaf book containing a page for each of his customers. The pages are not arranged alphabetically but are in the order in which customers are served on the route. From the deliverymen's loose-leaf books, clerks get the information needed for the office account cards and for preparing the biweekly bills. Each customer is assigned a number in the various loose-leaf books, and the same number is placed on the customer's account card. These office account cards are filed numerically. Do you think an alphabetic system would be an improvement?

4. The printed bill form that the National Milk Company uses for its customers is divided into two portions. The left side, which the customer is supposed to keep for his records, bears his name and address, itemizes what he purchased, and states the total amount he owes. The right side, which the customer is supposed to mail with his remittance, lists only the customer's account number and the total amount owed.

One of the accountants has complained that when a customer sends in the wrong half, time is lost because reference must be made to the card index to locate the account number. What would you suggest to eliminate this difficulty?

Subject Filing

SUBJECT FILING is the arrangement of records by names of items rather than by names of people, companies, or locations.

Subject files are set up with guides and folders, or guides and cards, the same as alphabetic correspondence or card files. But the captions are subjects instead of names of people or organizations. For example, the major captions of a subject file in a furniture store might be *Appliances, Bedroom Furniture, Carpets, Dining Room Furniture, Living Room Furniture,* and *Outdoor Furniture.* The major captions in part of an insurance company subject file might be *Changes, Claims, Collections, Collision Insurance, Comprehensive Insurance,* and *Costs.* In the files of a small organization, the subject captions are often merged with name captions. Hence, a radio repair shop might have in one file drawer folders with these captions: *Electronic Supply Company* (company name), *Electronic Tests* (subject), and *Elkton Radio Wholesalers* (company name). The departments of numerous big corporations maintain separate alphabetic and subject files. For example, one large corporation has an accounting department in which accounts are organized alphabetically by customer name. The same department maintains another file containing such subject captions as *Accruals, Allocations, Allowances,* and *Audits.*

When Subject Filing Is Used

Some records, such as inventory cards, lend themselves to subject organization because they refer primarily to items. Other papers—insurance policies are a good example—may be filed by name, number, *or* subject. Still others, such as checks, cannot be arranged on a subject basis at all, because they do not refer to a subject. Following are several situations in which records are organized by subject.

1. *When the records do not refer to the name of a person or an organization.* The inventory records of a wholesale candy company, for example, may be organized according to the kinds of candy products: *Bulk Candies, Candy Bars, Fancy Chocolates, Glacés,* etc.

2. *When it is likely that the records will be called for by subject.* The advertising manager of a leather goods company will probably ask his secretary for "the advertising contract on our new line of briefcases" instead of "the Globe Advertising Agency contract" or "our Contract No. 5-279 dated March 4." The contract will best be filed, then, under the subject heading *Advertising—Contracts—Briefcases.*

3. *When all the records about one product or activity are likely to be needed at one time.* The sales manager of a boat manufacturing firm, for example, will want all available information about a new Model J-2000 sailboat before he plans the sales campaign for that model. If the information is widely dispersed—filed under the names of parts suppliers, designers, and subcontractors—the file worker will have to search the entire file. With a subject filing system, however, the file worker would need to look only under *Sailboats—Model J-2000,* lift the folder from the drawer, and present it to the sales manager for immediate action.

4. *When records might otherwise become minutely subdivided.* To illustrate, a wholesale pharmaceutical dealer might purchase drugs from hundreds of different suppliers, but there might be only a small volume of correspondence, such as descriptive literature and price lists, concerning each supplier. Cumbersome alphabetic files could result from the many firm names involved. The wholesale dealer might better organize his files on a subject basis, using only a dozen major categories of drugs, such as *Antibiotics* and *Antiseptics,* as his main headings. Thus the records would be filed according to product and could be rapidly located. To provide a list of suppliers and the drugs they sell, only an alphabetic card index would be needed.

Kinds of Subject Files

The principal kinds of subject files are combination subject, alphabetic subject, and numeric subject.

Combination Subject Files.   A combination subject file contains subject captions mixed in with individual or company name captions.   This kind of subject file is used when there is relatively little material to be organized on a subject basis.   In such a case it is impractical to set up a separate subject file; so the subject captions, as described earlier in this chapter, are merged with name captions in what would otherwise be an alphabetic correspondence file.   A combination subject file is illustrated below.

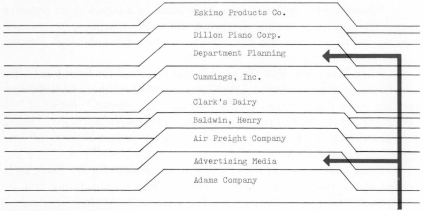

Portion of a combination subject file.   Arrows point to subject folders interfiled with folders for individual and company names.

Alphabetic Subject Files.   Alphabetic subject files are similar to alphabetic correspondence files except that all of the captions refer to things instead of people and organizations.   There are two arrangements for alphabetic subject files—encyclopedic and dictionary.

A subject file with *encyclopedic arrangement* has alphabetized major headings, which in turn have alphabetized divisions and subdivisions.   For example, the captions listed below might be among the headings, divisions, and subdivisions in the subject files of Wholesale Grocery Suppliers.

CAPTIONS	EXPLANATION
Breads	First heading
Biscuits	First division of Breads
Loaf Bread	Second division of Breads
Rye	First subdivision of Loaf Bread
Wheat	Second subdivision of Loaf Bread
White	Third subdivision of Loaf Bread
Rolls	Third division of Breads
Sweet Rolls	Fourth division of Breads
Candies	Second heading
Bulk Candies	First division of Candies
Candy Bars	Second division of Candies
Fancy Chocolates	Third division of Candies

In the encyclopedic arrangement on page 104, one file worker might look for information concerning sweet rolls under *Breads*, where he would find it, yet another file worker might look for the same information under *Desserts*, where he would not. It is therefore necessary to create an alphabetic list of all the captions in a subject file that has encyclopedic arrangement. This list (or file of cards) is called a *relative index* and includes all the headings, divisions, and subdivisions in the file. It serves the same purpose as the index of a book. The file worker who wants information about sweet rolls but who is not certain under what heading it is filed would first look under the *S*'s in the relative index, as is shown below.

Salad Dressing	Spices & Dressings--Salad Dressing
Sausage	Meats--Pork--Sausage
Sour Cream	Dairy Products--Cream
Sweet Rolls	Breads--Sweet Rolls

Besides listing the headings, divisions, and subdivisions of the file, a good relative index will also list topics related to the actual captions in the file. A file worker would thus be referred to the proper caption regardless of the name for a topic that comes to his mind. For example, if there is a folder labeled *Carpets* in the files of a furniture store, the relative index, if properly prepared, will list *Carpets* and also such related topics as *Rugs* and *Floor Coverings*, even though there is no folder for the latter two topics. These related topics would refer the file worker to the appropriate folder, as is shown below.

Floor Coverings	<u>See</u> Carpets

Rugs	<u>See</u> Carpets

A relative index, then, can serve as a cross-reference for related topics as well as a direct reference to the captions in the subject file.

A subject file with *dictionary arrangement* has no divisions and subdivisions of subjects. Because the subjects are arranged in alphabetic sequence like the words in a dictionary, a relative index is not necessary. This type of alphabetic subject file is used in small businesses and other situations in which division of topics is not desired. One example of dictionary subject arrangement is the listing of types of businesses in the classified section, or yellow pages, of a telephone directory.

Alphabetic Subject File with Dictionary Arrangement

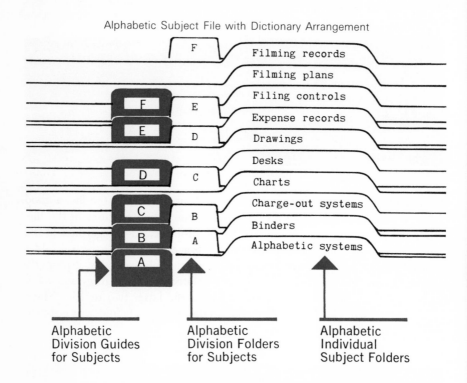

Numeric Subject Files. Numeric subject filing has the advantages of any numeric filing system. Coding is much easier than with alphabetic subject systems because only a number, and not a long subject caption, is recorded on the record. The files are easier to expand because new topics can be placed at the end of the files rather than inserted in the middle, as with alphabetic files. Because all topics have a code number, they do not have to be arranged in alphabetic order. Therefore, another important advantage of numeric subject filing is that related topics can be placed conveniently near each other in the files without regard to alphabetic sequence. Of course, a card index is needed for numeric subject systems, just as it was needed for the numeric systems discussed in Chapter 6.

Three important types of numeric subject systems are simple-numeric, decimal-numeric, and duplex-numeric.

Simple-numeric subject systems usually have three-digit captions. The main headings are usually hundreds and are assigned first, as in this example of a system the Wholesale Grocery Suppliers might set up:

Breads	100	Fruits	500
Candies	200	Meats	600
Dairy Products	300	Spices & Dressings	700
Desserts	400	Vegetables	800

Then the divisions of each heading are assigned numbers that are hundreds and tens. For example:

Dairy Products	300
Butter	310
Cheese	320
Cream	330
Eggs	340
Milk	350

Finally, the subdivisions of each division are assigned numbers. Thus:

Milk	350
Buttermilk	351
Chocolate Milk	352
Skim Milk	353
Whole Milk	354

Notice that some numbers are not assigned, such as 900, 360, and 355. This allows for expansion in the event that new headings, divisions, or subdivisions are added later. The assigned numbers are placed on guides and folders in the file, sometimes together with the subject caption, sometimes alone.

A card is prepared for each heading, division, and subdivision in the file. The cards are arranged alphabetically to provide a reference for the code numbers assigned. The card for *Whole Milk* is shown below as an example. It would be filed under "W" in an alphabetic card index.

Alphabetic Index Card

Whole Milk   354

Decimal-numeric subject systems permit more subdivisions than simple-numeric systems. Up to the first subdivision, the decimal-numeric code numbers are the same as the simple-numeric codes, as:

Cream	330.
Sweet Cream	331.
Sour Cream	332.

The code 331. (Sweet Cream) can be further subdivided by adding one digit to the right of the decimal point, as:

Sweet Cream	331.
Heavy	331.1
Light	331.2

It is possible to continue the subdivisions by adding more digits to the right of a decimal point. The number 331.2 could be subdivided into 331.21, 331.22, 331.23, etc.

A Decimal-Numeric Subject File

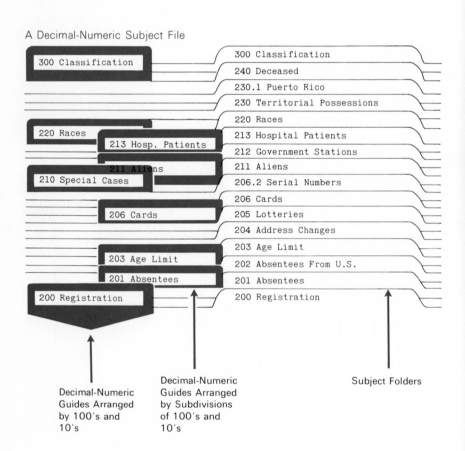

Duplex-numeric subject systems, which use a number, a dash, and a second number, permit more than ten main headings and more than nine divisions under any one heading. (Simple-numeric and decimal-numeric systems are limited to ten main headings, 000–900, and nine main divisions under any one heading—110–190, for example.) Further subdivisions are possible with the duplex-numeric systems by adding a hyphen and beginning a new series of numbers. Some duplex-numeric systems use a combination of numbers and letters of the alphabet. The chart below shows how a main heading and its eleven divisions would be assigned codes in both simple-numeric and duplex-numeric systems. Note that the tenth and eleventh divisions cannot be coded in the simple-numeric system.

SUBJECT	SIMPLE-NUMERIC	DUPLEX-NUMERIC
Vegetables	800	8
Beans	810	8-1
Beets	820	8-2
Cabbage	830	8-3
Carrots	840	8-4
Lettuce	850	8-5
Peas	860	8-6
Potatoes	870	8-7
Radishes	880	8-8
Spinach	890	8-9
Squash	No provision	8-10
Turnips	No provision	8-11

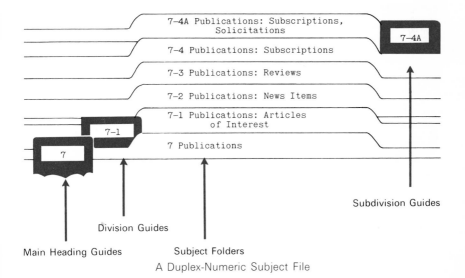

A Duplex-Numeric Subject File

Example of a Subject File

Probably no two subject filing systems are exactly the same. There are variations in captions and in the type and organization of filed materials. Even so, it is helpful in studying subject filing to see how a sample subject file is used in an actual situation. Let us examine the system used by the 135 county agricultural extension offices of the state of Virginia.

These extension offices are spread throughout the state and are operated by county agents whose job is to teach better methods of farming and rural living to the people of the counties. In order to help the agents carry out this task, the Virginia Agricultural Experiment Station and the U. S. Department of Agriculture continually supply the agents with current information. The information is in the form of letters, news releases, bulletins, pamphlets and brochures, research reports, and miscellaneous forms and documents. The material must be organized so that the agents can quickly locate facts needed to solve numerous farming and other rural problems.

The filing system that has been adopted for the county agents is known as the Subject-Numeric System of Classifying and Filing. This system is an adaptation of both the alphabetic subject and duplex-numeric systems. It includes the alphabetic arrangement of 31 major headings shown in the list below:

Administration	Dairy Science
Agronomy	Economics
Animal Husbandry	Engineering
Associations and Organizations	Entomology and Plant Pathology
Clothing	Events
Communications—Public Relations	Extension Education—Training
Extension Programs	Horticulture
Family Life	Housing
Farm and Home Development	Poultry Husbandry
Foods and Nutrition	Recreation
Forestry	Reports and Statistics
4-H Clubs	Rural Arts
Health and Safety	Rural Development
Home Demonstration	Sociology
Home Furnishings	Wildlife
Home Management	

For each of the major headings there are several divisions, which are assigned consecutive numbers to speed coding, filing, and finding. For example, the major heading *Agronomy* is divided as follows:

Agronomy
  1 Crops
  2 Soils
  3 Weeds

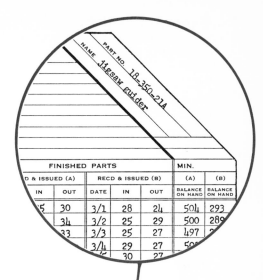

| PART NO. 18-350-21A |
| NAME jigsaw guider |

FINISHED PARTS				MIN.	
D & ISSUED (A)		RECD & ISSUED (B)			(A)	(B)
IN	OUT	DATE	IN	OUT	BALANCE ON HAND	BALANCE ON HAND
5	30	3/1	28	24	504	293
	34	3/2	25	29	500	289
	33	3/3	25	27	497	2
		3/4	29	27	50	
			30	27		

This subject file for inventory records is organized by part number.

The divisions can in turn be subdivided. The subdivisions are assigned numbers in the same manner as in a duplex-numeric system. To illustrate, the division *Crops* is subdivided as follows:

1 Crops
   1-1 Cash and Feed Crops
   1-2 Hay and Forage Crops
   1-3 Pasture
   1-4 Seed

All of the headings, divisions, and subdivisions are placed on guides that have tabs in one of three positions, as illustrated below.

The straight-edge folders are also labeled with the appropriate captions. Straight-edge folders for main headings and divisions are labeled at the left, and straight-edge folders for subdivisions are labeled at both the left and the right.

An idea of how a file drawer looks when filled is also provided by the illustration below.

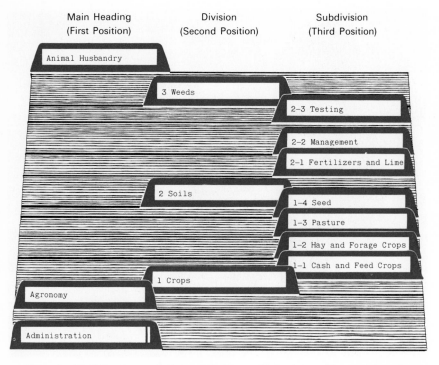

Part of a filled file drawer is illustrated above.   Note the positions of the tabs.

As you learned earlier, this arrangement of a subject file (encyclopedic) requires a relative index. Here is a portion of the one for this system:

REFERENCE	CAPTION
Accessories, Clothing	Clothing 5-1
Accessories, Home Furnishings	Home Furnishings 4-1
Accessories, Lawn	See: Horticulture 1
Accounting	See: Administration
Accounts, Farm	Economics 1-3
Achievement Day, 4-H	See: 4-H Clubs 1
Activities, 4-H	4-H Clubs 1
Agreements, Farm	Economics 1-5
Agricultural Engineering	See: Engineering

Procedure for Cross-Referencing in a Subject Correspondence System

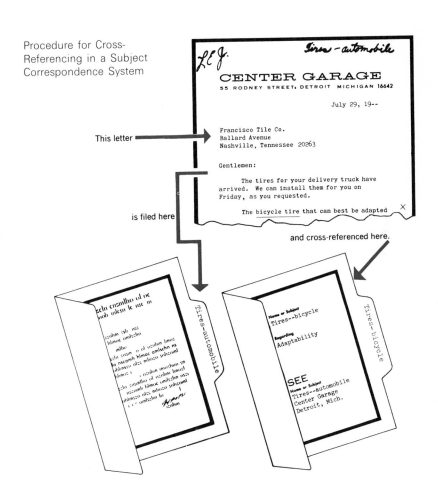

This letter

is filed here

and cross-referenced here.

Steps in the Subject Filing of Correspondence

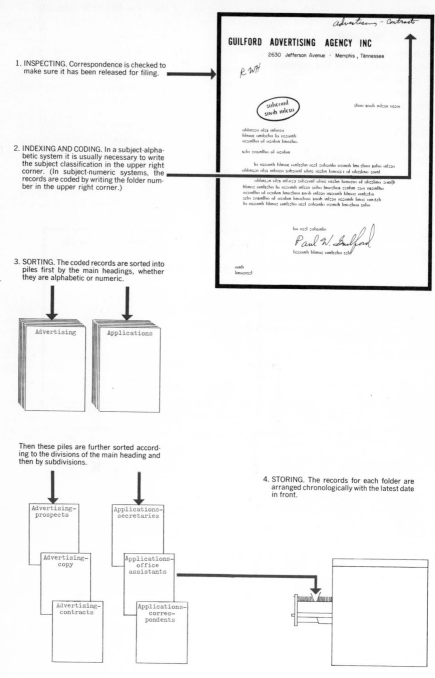

1. INSPECTING. Correspondence is checked to make sure it has been released for filing.

2. INDEXING AND CODING. In a subject-alphabetic system it is usually necessary to write the subject classification in the upper right corner. (In subject-numeric systems, the records are coded by writing the folder number in the upper right corner.)

3. SORTING. The coded records are sorted into piles first by the main headings, whether they are alphabetic or numeric.

Then these piles are further sorted according to the divisions of the main heading and then by subdivisions.

4. STORING. The records for each folder are arranged chronologically with the latest date in front.

As you can see, the relative index of this filing system includes not only the captions in the file but also related topics, which are referred to the captions by the word *See*. The relative index thus acts as a cross-reference. The relative index is kept on cards, each reference having a separate card.

This subject filing system also includes a provision for cross-referencing within the subject folders. If a record refers to more than one subject, it is filed under the most important subject and cross-referenced under the others. A standard cross-reference sheet is used for this purpose.

Subject Correspondence Filing Procedure. A general procedure for subject correspondence filing is outlined on page 114. This procedure can be adapted to the many variations that are possible in organizing records by subject.

Because subject captions are not always apparent, the indexing of correspondence by subject is more difficult than indexing by individual or company name. Often the indexing step is performed by the executive who handles the correspondence. If the indexing is performed by a file clerk, the relative index is frequently consulted to determine the exact folder caption under which the correspondence is to be filed. If a piece of correspondence refers to more than one subject, a cross-reference sheet is prepared for the secondary subject, as illustrated on page 113.

Questions and Problems

1. What is subject filing?
2. When should subject filing be used?
3. What are the three basic kinds of subject files?
4. When is a combination subject file used? What would the captions be?
5. What is the difference between the encyclopedic arrangement and the dictionary arrangement of an alphabetic subject file?
6. What is the purpose of a relative index?
7. What are some of the advantages of numeric subject filing?
8. Compare the organization of a simple-numeric, decimal-numeric, and duplex-numeric file. What is the advantage of each?
9. How are records cross-referenced in subject filing?
10. How are records coded in subject filing?
11. Enumerate and describe the steps in the subject filing procedure.

Case Problems in Records Management

1. The Master Auto Supply Company operates a chain of stores selling automobile parts and accessories. They use a subject filing system in which records of suppliers are filed according to the articles they manufacture. The purchasing department complains of difficulty in locating records when the name of a company, but not the product, is known. What can be done to eliminate this difficulty?

2. The various articles manufactured by the Crescent Electric Supply Company include many parts with similar names but different sizes and shapes. What method of identification and what type of filing system do you recommend? Be specific in your suggestions for the primary and secondary captions.

3. The Thomas and Greenwood Company has a large turnover in its office staff. The new employees have considerable difficulty in using the subject files. What can the file supervisor do to alleviate this?

4. The Lawrence Company uses a subject filing system. All the work in connection with filing, including the coding, has been performed in the filing department. The following proposal has been placed in the suggestion box for reducing confusion about the subject categories used for storing records: "Inasmuch as the department receiving an incoming letter is the one most likely to refer to it again after it has been stored, the coding should be done by that department rather than by the filing department." Do you think this suggestion should be adopted? Give your reasons.

Geographic Filing

GEOGRAPHIC FILING is an alphabetic arrangement of records—first according to location, then according to name or subject.

Suppose that Mr. Curtis Martin of the Texas Real Estate Company gets a telephone call inquiring about houses available in Brownsville. He consults the Brownsville section of the files and finds an offer by John Thompson to sell his home. As a result, Mr. Martin makes a sale. Mr. Thompson's house was listed behind a guide bearing the caption "Brownsville" because Mr. Martin usually receives calls for property according to its location. Therefore, records about this property are stored according to location, or geographically. Other Brownsville properties listed for sale are arranged alphabetically behind the Brownsville guide according to the names of the sellers.

Businesses that use geographic filing include sales organizations in which men are responsible for definite geographic areas, mail-order businesses in which a geographic arrangement of customer names provides a mailing list that is arranged by state and town to speed the sorting of outgoing mailings, and public utilities that divide the areas they serve into geographic districts and have a branch office in each.

Organization of a Geographic File

Geographic files, of course, are not all organized in the same way. An automobile manufacturer, for example, may use names of nations for the major divisions in the file.   But a state department of agriculture might use towns or counties.   Among the many factors that will determine how a geographic file will be set up are (1) the type of business, (2) how the records will be used, and (3) the geographic areas in which the company does business. Regardless of the differences, you can readily understand most geographic filing systems if you are familiar with a typical one.

Looking Into a Geographic File.   Let us see how the contents of a typical file drawer, such as the one illustrated on page 119, are arranged (1) looking from front to back and (2) looking at the position of the tabs from left to right.

1. Looking from front to back:
   a. In the front is a guide covering a major segment of the file.   This is called a *state guide,* and its tab has the caption *Massachusetts.*
   b. Behind the state guide is an *alphabetic guide,* and its tab has the caption *A.*   It covers all cities in Massachusetts beginning with *A.*
   c. Behind the alphabetic guide is a *town or city guide* for the town of *Athol.*
   d. Behind the town guide are *individual folders* for correspondents in *Athol.*
   e. Behind the individual folders is a *town or city miscellaneous folder,* and its tab has the caption *Athol* for correspondents in Athol who do not warrant an individual folder.
   f. Behind the town miscellaneous folder is a *state miscellaneous folder* with the caption *A* for towns in Massachusetts beginning with *A* that do not warrant a town or city miscellaneous folder.   For example, correspondence pertaining to Adams, Massachusetts, would be stored in the *A* state miscellaneous folder.
2. Looking at the position of the tabs from left to right:
   First position: *State guides* and *alphabetic guides*
   Second position: *Town or city guides*
   Third position: *Town or city miscellaneous folders* and *state miscellaneous folders*
   Fourth position: *Individual folders.*   (The caption gives the name of the town or city first, the state second, and then the correspondent.   The town is listed before the state because the town guide is nearby, making cross-checking easy.)
   Fifth position: *Special guides* and *out guides*

Sometimes, when there is a large volume of correspondence for one town or city, the correspondence in a town or city miscellaneous folder is alphabetically subdivided.   In the illustration, for example, *Boston* has been subdivided so that there are five miscellaneous folders for Boston, each for a different alphabetic group.   There is a guide for each of the subdivided folders.

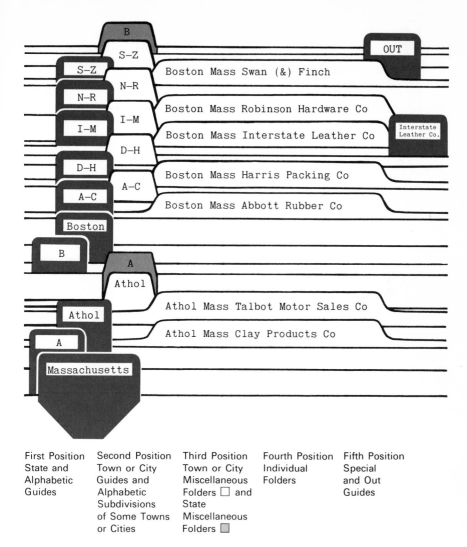

First Position	Second Position	Third Position	Fourth Position	Fifth Position
State and Alphabetic Guides	Town or City Guides and Alphabetic Subdivisions of Some Towns or Cities	Town or City Miscellaneous Folders ☐ and State Miscellaneous Folders ◻	Individual Folders	Special and Out Guides

A geographic file showing the arrangement of guide and folder tabs from left to right. Notice that the miscellaneous folder for Boston has been alphabetically subdivided into five separate folders to prevent overcrowding.

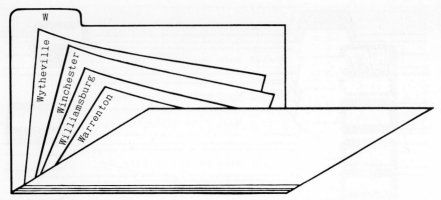

1. Records pertaining to miscellaneous towns within a state are stored in the state miscellaneous folders. The above folder is for miscellaneous towns in Virginia with names that begin with *W*.

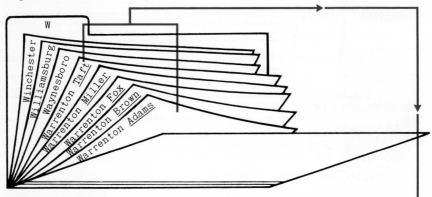

2. When enough records pertaining to one town or city have accumulated in the state miscellaneous folder. . .

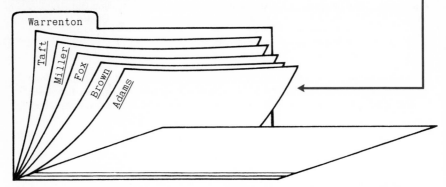

3. a town or city miscellaneous folder is opened for that town or city. If this folder becomes overcrowded, it may be alphabetically subdivided as was done with the folder for Boston in the illustration on page 119.

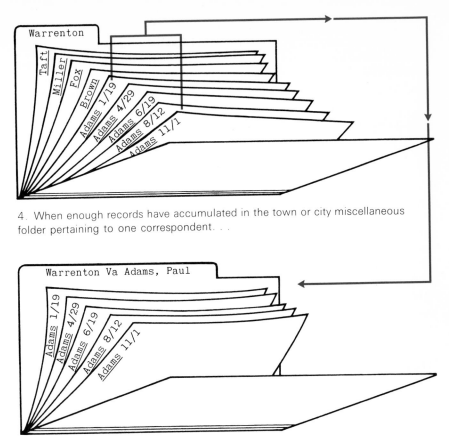

4. When enough records have accumulated in the town or city miscellaneous folder pertaining to one correspondent. . .

5. an individual folder is opened for that correspondent.

Arrangement of Records in Folders. Within the individual folders in a geographic file, records are arranged chronologically, with the record bearing the latest date in front. In the town or city miscellaneous folders, records are arranged alphabetically first by the names of the correspondents and then chronologically for each correspondent. In the state miscellaneous folders, records are arranged first alphabetically by the name of the town or city, then alphabetically by the name of the correspondent, and finally chronologically for each correspondent. The five steps that a record might undergo in a geographic file, beginning with the state miscellaneous folder, are illustrated on this page and the preceding page.

Auxiliary Card Index. It is possible that a file worker would be asked for the Clay Products Company folder without being told the geographic location of the company. Or he might be asked for correspondence pertaining to

Mr. Charles Bashaw of that company. Unless the file worker had a very good memory, he might not know in which section of the files to look for the folder. For that reason, an auxiliary card index is often used with a geographic filing system. The cards are arranged alphabetically by the names of the correspondents, and they indicate the geographic location of the correspondents.

Geographic Cross-Referencing

If a letter from Swan & Finch of Boston refers to Clay Products Company of Athol, it is likely that the original letter would be stored in the Swan & Finch folder and a cross-reference sheet, as shown below, or a photocopy of the letter would be stored in the Clay Products Company folder.

When there is a permanent and recurrent cross-reference, instead of a cross-reference sheet, a manila tabbed cross-reference form is used. For example, if the Adams Construction Company has main offices in Memphis and branch offices in Bristol, Knoxville, and Nashville, it may be desirable to group all the correspondence in the Memphis folder. Then cross-reference forms with tabs referring to Memphis would be placed behind the Bristol, Knoxville, and Nashville guides. This cross-reference form is illustrated below.

Steps in Geographic Correspondence Filing

The steps in geographic correspondence filing are illustrated on page 123.

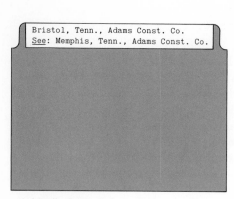

Bristol, Tenn., Adams Const. Co.
<u>See</u>: Memphis, Tenn., Adams Const. Co.

A Manila Tabbed Cross-Reference Form

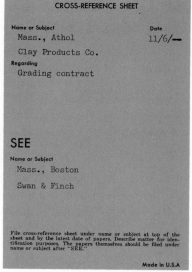

CROSS-REFERENCE SHEET

Name or Subject   Date
 Mass., Athol   11/6/—
 Clay Products Co.
Regarding
 Grading contract

SEE

Name or Subject
 Mass., Boston
 Swan & Finch

File cross-reference sheet under name or subject at top of the sheet and by the latest date of papers. Describe matter for identification purposes. The papers themselves should be filed under name or subject after "SEE."

Made in U.S.A

A Geographic Cross-Reference Sheet

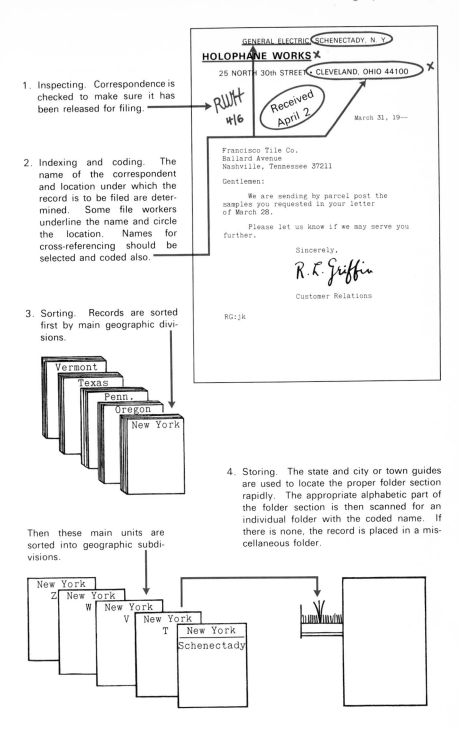

1. Inspecting. Correspondence is checked to make sure it has been released for filing.

2. Indexing and coding. The name of the correspondent and location under which the record is to be filed are determined. Some file workers underline the name and circle the location. Names for cross-referencing should be selected and coded also.

3. Sorting. Records are sorted first by main geographic divisions.

Then these main units are sorted into geographic subdivisions.

4. Storing. The state and city or town guides are used to locate the proper folder section rapidly. The appropriate alphabetic part of the folder section is then scanned for an individual folder with the coded name. If there is none, the record is placed in a miscellaneous folder.

Geographic Card Files

Geographic filing is often used for card records. For example, a realtor might keep a card file of houses for rent, arranged by location in a city. A utility company might keep a card file of customers arranged by street name and number. Salesmen frequently keep card records concerning their clients, and these may be arranged primarily by city, town, or county name. Charitable organizations frequently organize pledge cards and other records by territory so that personal follow-up may be made with minimum difficulty. In each case, it is wise to keep a separate alphabetic list or card index of the names that have been organized geographically. With an index, the cards filed geographically can be located if the name of the person or company is known but the address or location is not.

Questions and Problems

1. What is geographic filing?
2. Name some businesses that use geographic filing.
3. What determines how a business organizes its geographic file?
4. Name some divisions and subdivisions that could be used for primary and secondary guide captions in a geographic file.
5. Describe one possible arrangement of guides and folders from front to back and from left to right in a geographic file drawer.
6. In what order is information listed on the caption of a geographic individual folder?
7. What are the two types of miscellaneous folders in a geographic file, and for what is each used?
8. What is done when a miscellaneous town or city folder becomes overcrowded?
9. How is correspondence arranged within a geographic individual folder? within each type of miscellaneous folder?
10. Describe how a record might progress from a state miscellaneous folder, to a town or city miscellaneous folder, and finally to an individual folder.
11. For what purpose is a card index used in a geographic file?
12. How can cross-referencing be done in a geographic file?
13. Enumerate and describe the steps in the geographic filing procedure.
14. Under what circumstances might card files be organized geographically?

Case Problems in Records Management

1. The John Lindstrom Company uses an alphabetic filing system. Analysis of the company's activities reveals that record handling could be speeded up if some provision were made for geographic filing. It is estimated that approximately 75 percent of the records would be called for by correspondents' names and the remaining 25 percent by geographic loca-

tion. How would you reorganize the files? Be specific in your recommendations, stating what you would have as primary, secondary, and other guides, and what you would have as individual and miscellaneous folders.

2. The Henderson Company, a nationwide distributor of electrical equipment, now has two types of miscellaneous folders in its geographic file: town or city and state. One of the file clerks has suggested that the state miscellaneous folders be eliminated. If you were the file supervisor, would you adopt the suggestion?

3. The J. R. Logan Company files most of its customer records geographically. However, the records of some customers who do a large volume of business are stored in a separate alphabetic file. Do you think such a system leads to filing efficiency? Why?

4. The R. J. Lloyd Company operates within the boundaries of New York State. Ninety percent of its business is conducted in the cities of Albany, Schenectady, and Troy. The remainder is done in the 25 cities, towns, and villages listed below. What primary and secondary guide captions should the company decide upon when it sets up its geographic filing system?

a. Niskayuna	j. Green Island	r. Defreestville
b. Latham	k. Guilderland	s. Eagle Mills
c. Newtonville	l. South Schenectady	t. Guilderland Center
d. Loudonville	m. Scotia	u. Vischer Ferry
e. Menands	n. Crescent	v. Waterville
f. Colonie	o. Elsmere	w. Brunswick Center
g. Fullers	p. Delmar	x. Dunnsville
h. Waterford	q. Rensselaer	y. Slingerlands
i. Cohoes		

Equipment
and Supplies

DOZENS OF MANUFACTURERS offer almost every conceivable type, size, price, and design of cabinets, supplies, and special equipment for housing and managing records. Made-to-order equipment is also available for unique systems. Office equipment exhibits, catalogs of manufacturers, office management magazines, and showrooms of stationers, business-equipment dealers, and office furniture stores are excellent sources of up-to-date information. New filing products are placed on the market often. Office workers and supervisors who are concerned with records management should keep constantly in touch with new developments. Only by doing so can they keep their filing systems efficient, flexible, and easy to operate.

Aside from considerations of what records should be kept where and by what method, the efficiency of a records management system will depend on the equipment and supplies used. To be efficient, the system must:

1. *Save time.* This means that equipment and supplies must be designed so that those who handle records do not go through unnecessary motions.
2. *Provide adequate protection of records.* Some files should have locks to safeguard their contents; others should be fireproof. The importance of the records, then, needs to be considered when purchasing equipment.
3. *Conserve space.* Because of today's high rental rates, construction costs of new buildings, and maintenance expenses, files should be designed so that they do not take up more space than is absolutely necessary for an efficient system.

High Value of Quality

The relative cost of maintaining a standard four-drawer correspondence file, illustrated on this page, is only one bit of evidence of the importance of selecting high-quality housing for all records. Although the percentages in the illustration vary according to the geographical section of the country, it is apparent that labor cost is by far the biggest filing expense. Therefore, any feature of equipment or supplies that significantly increases the worker's production and efficiency deserves special attention on the purchaser's part.

In selecting files, labor costs should be kept in mind as well as the ability of the files to protect records from misfiling, theft, fire, and other causes of loss. It is very difficult to assign a value to the records in a file. The creation cost of a contract may be only a few dollars. However, if the contract is destroyed or lost, it might mean the loss of thousands of dollars. There are many vital records—such as financial records, formulas, deeds—that are more essential to business survival than are the physical assets of the company. Therefore, any feature that will significantly improve protection also makes

ANNUAL COST OF MAINTAINING A FOUR-DRAWER FILE

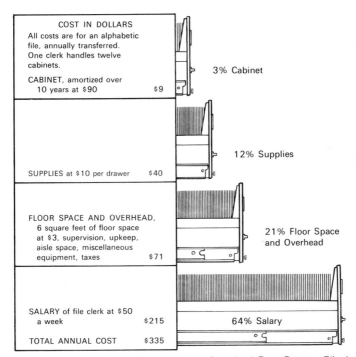

COST IN DOLLARS	
All costs are for an alphabetic file, annually transferred. One clerk handles twelve cabinets.	
CABINET, amortized over 10 years at $90	$9

3% Cabinet

SUPPLIES at $10 per drawer	$40

12% Supplies

FLOOR SPACE AND OVERHEAD, 6 square feet of floor space at $3, supervision, upkeep, aisle space, miscellaneous equipment, taxes	$71

21% Floor Space and Overhead

SALARY of file clerk at $50 a week	$215
TOTAL ANNUAL COST	$335

64% Salary

How the Relative Cost of Maintaining a Standard Four-Drawer File Is Distributed

the equipment or supply more worthy of purchase. Although money should not be squandered in the purchase of equipment and supplies, neither should false economy be practiced. Out of the many types and grades of equipment and supplies available, there is "a right item for the job."

Correspondence Files

Today, the great majority of file cabinets are constructed of steel. Some are lined with asbestos to provide fire resistance. Locks of either the key or combination types are available for some files for the protection of valuable papers, and good-quality file drawers have safety latches so that drawers will open only when a lever near the handle is pressed. Also available are special compact file cabinets that have five drawers in approximately the same space as the standard four-drawer cabinet.

Correspondence file cabinets are available in many grades. Businesses have found that the best-quality equipment is usually the most economical over a number of years. A letter-size file drawer when full carries a load of 60

Courtesy Columbia-Hallowell Division of Standard Pressed Steel Company

This modern, good-looking file cabinet has recessed drawer handles.

to 70 pounds. Therefore, drawers should have telescoping slides to furnish support when the drawers are fully extended. The slides themselves should move on ball-bearing or nylon rollers so that drawers can be opened and closed easily with one hand. The inside frame of the cabinet should be rigidly braced.

File drawers are not always completely filled, so records within them must be held upright by some device other than the back of the drawer. In addition, records that are firmly packed together are less subject to damage by fire than loosely packed records. (Have you ever tried to burn a thick catalog or directory?) *Follower blocks,* or *compressors* as they are sometimes called, are used to support and to compress records. They move forward and backward in the file drawer, yet lock in the desired position to hold records. Followers should be strong but not so bulky that they occupy valuable filing space. So that guides will not accidentally be lifted out of the drawer when folders

IMPORTANT FEATURES OF GOOD-QUALITY FILE CABINETS

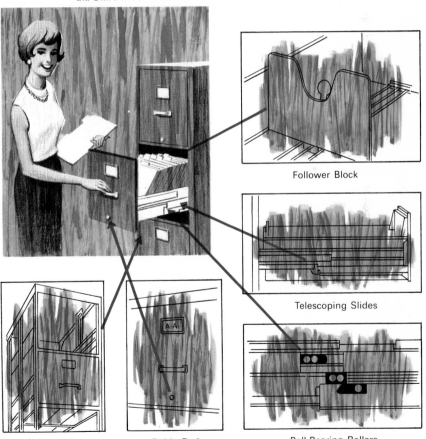

Follower Block

Telescoping Slides

Reinforced Frame　　　　Guide Rod　　　　Ball-Bearing Rollers

Verti-Swing
Hanging Folders

Courtesy The Globe-Wernicke Co.

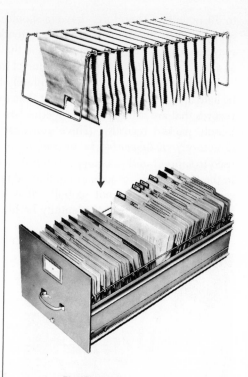

FlexiFile with Cloth Pockets

Courtesy Remington Rand

Super-Filer with Drop Front
and Self-Adjusting Dividers

Courtesy General Fireproofing Co.

These files have special features to increase filing efficiency.

are removed, there should be some means of anchoring the guides in place. Most file drawers have guide rods that are inserted through holes in one or more projections at the bottom or sides of the guides. This keeps guides in the drawer but permits them to move forward and backward along the rods.

If papers are packed too tightly in file drawers, they will become wrinkled and unsightly, folders and guides will be short-lived, and file workers will have difficulty removing and replacing records. To prevent such difficulties, some filing cabinets provide V-shaped working space. This working space is provided in some models by a drop front that eases the tension on the tops of the records when the drawer is opened and compresses the records when the drawer is closed. Other models have a hinged back for the same purposes. Both types have the additional advantages of more storage capacity per square foot of floor space than conventional cabinets and greater fire protection due to the automatic compression of records when drawers are closed.

Besides the traditional drawer-type file, correspondence can be stored in open-shelf files, in electrically operated files that raise or lower a group of records to a comfortable filing position, or in *rocking compartment* files, which resemble steel bookcases when they are closed.

This electrically operated file saves time and motion by positioning files at desk level within seconds.

CORRESPONDENCE FILING SPACE CHART

Item	Average Filing Space Required
175 pieces of correspondence	1″
25 guides (medium weight)	$^7/_8$″
100 individual folders (medium weight)	$2^1/_4$″
25 miscellaneous folders (medium weight)	$^1/_2$″

In deciding how many drawers or cabinets to purchase, it is necessary to determine the quantity of material to be filed. The chart shown above can then be used to estimate the number of inches (measured from front to back inside the drawer) of filing space that will be needed. By dividing into this figure the filing inches in one drawer, the number of file drawers needed will be known. Correspondence files have between 24 and 27 inches of filing space, but about 4 inches should be subtracted for working space. For example, if the chart shows that the filed materials will occupy 1,000 inches, and there are 24 inches of filing space in each drawer of the cabinets to be purchased, then the number of cabinets that will be needed is figured as follows:

Filing inches in each drawer	24
Minus inches allowed for working space	−4
Inches of space to be used in each drawer	20
Inches of space all records will use	1,000
Divide by space to be used in each drawer	1,000 ÷ 20 = 50 drawers
Number of drawers needed	50 drawers ÷ 4 or 5 =
Number of cabinets is then figured by dividing number of drawers per cabinet into number needed.	10 five-drawer or 13 four-drawer cabinets

A Vertical File for Punched Cards

Special Filing Cabinets

Filing cabinets are available for storing checks, legal documents, catalogs, 5- by 3- or 6- by 4-inch cards, punched cards, punched tapes, magnetic tapes, blueprints, microfilms, microfiche, X-rays, fingerprints. In short, there is a cabinet to house nearly every standard-size record.

Even though the four-drawer correspondence file is the most popular, cabinets are made in several drawer heights for special purposes: one or two drawers for filing while seated at a desk, three drawers for counters, and five and six drawers for space saving. Files can be arranged in sections to form work alcoves or partitions. To permit flexibility, drawer dividers are obtainable for partitioning a drawer in any way desired.

For seldom-used transferred records, cabinets of inexpensive construction are practical. Some are made of corrugated fiberboard; some are of lightweight metal; others are a combination of the two. Drawer-type transfer files usually have only one drawer per unit. These units can usually be interlocked to form sturdy batteries of files twelve or more drawers high. Less expensive transfer files open from the top like ordinary boxes.

As pointed out in Chapter 4, there is a wide variety of card and visible filing equipment—rotary wheels, shelf trays, rotary trays, horizontal drawers,

Courtesy Robert P. Gillotte Co., Inc.

This open-shelf file contains hanging pockets for the storage of a company's promotional materials.

The folders in this file are in random order. However, indexing a number on the keyboard causes the folder bearing that number to be automatically pushed partially forward for pickup.

This is a file for magnetic tapes for computers. Each tape container is labeled for indexing.

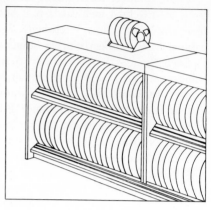

This file stores paper tapes in rolls.

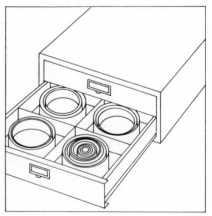

vertical compartments, and books. The type chosen depends upon the number of records to be stored and whether the records are to be used for reference or for recording of information.

Guides

Guides are the key to efficient vertical filing. Without them, records will not stand upright properly in the drawer. Guides also serve as signposts to speed finding and filing. The number of guides, the tab size and position, and the quality of construction depend on the filing system being used. They may be purchased in all standard correspondence drawer sizes as well as for

This work station has a built-in filing unit which can be used to house punched tapes, punched cards, or card records of other types.

drawers used in special systems, such as bank, hospital, and insurance company files. Guides made of manila stock or index bristol are inexpensive and will serve in transfer files or temporary card files. In active files, however, guides made of pressboard or fiber should be used. A standard 25-point (.025 inch) thickness of pressboard is durable and rigid enough to support records, yet flexible enough to resist dog-earing or breaking. In some card systems, guides made of plastic or lightweight metal are used.

Guides are produced with the tab or upper-edge projection in various sizes (cuts) and positions so that they can be adapted to any system. The tabs may be simply an extension of the guide with the caption printed or with a blank space for a label. Some tabs of this type are reinforced with transparent plastic. High-quality guides, however, have metal or plastic tabs that are riveted to the body of the guide. Such tabs usually have a slot for the insertion of a caption label under a transparent plastic window.

There are a number of other guide features and accessories. Angular tabs are slanted back for good visibility and are especially helpful in lower file drawers. There are even tabs that magnify the guide caption. Separate plastic tabs can be purchased in long strips and cut to the desired size for attachment to guides in any position. These may be used to replace broken tabs or to provide additional captions. Good-quality guides have metal-reinforced guide rod projections. As with filing cabinets, the best-quality

Guides and Tabs of Varying
Designs

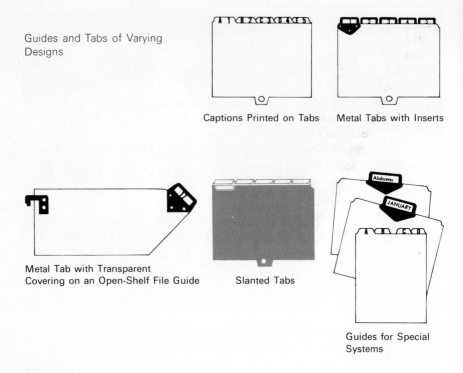

Captions Printed on Tabs　　Metal Tabs with Inserts

Metal Tab with Transparent
Covering on an Open-Shelf File Guide　　Slanted Tabs

Guides for Special
Systems

guides with the most useful features are usually worth the extra money because
they give lasting and efficient service.

Folders

Durable folders that have a minimum of thickness and a smooth surface
are needed for active correspondence files.　As is true with guides, folders
are available in several styles and types of material.　For average use, manila
and kraft folders provide good service and can be purchased in several weights;
the choice should depend upon the type and extent of handling.　Plastic folders
have the advantages of reusability and ease of filing.　For bulky papers or
for very heavy handling, fiber or pressboard folders with cloth expansion
hinges at the bottom should be used.　For checks and other small business
forms, transparent plastic folders may be the most appropriate.

Some folders have a double thickness along the top, which adds to their
life span without increasing the bulk of the file drawer.　Folders that are scored
along the bottom of the front flap can be expanded neatly.　As the number
of papers increases, a new fold is made along one of the scores.　This flattens
the bottom and permits all records to stand evenly and squarely on their edges.

Several types of folders are designed for special needs.　File pockets, also

Folders and Guides for Open-Shelf Files

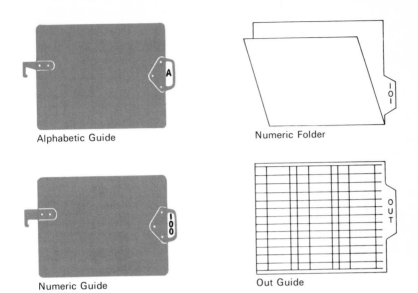

Alphabetic Guide

Numeric Folder

Numeric Guide

Out Guide

called envelope folders, are used for materials that are especially bulky or that are frequently taken away from the files. For case histories, medical records, and personnel records, folders that have dividers or compartments within them are frequently used. For follow-up work, folders with adjustable date signals are popular. Other folders that are available have built-in paper fasteners to keep records from accidentally sliding out.

Folder tabs are obtainable in nearly any cut or position desired. Tabs are generally an extension of the folder itself, but pressboard and fiber folders usually have metal or plastic tabs. For open-shelf files, tabs are on the side of guides and folders instead of the top.

Suspended, or *hanging,* folders are supported from their top edges by a metal frame within the file drawer. They do not rest on the bottom of the drawer. These folders save space because the follower blocks and guides can be eliminated (attachable tabs on the front of the folders can be used in the place of conventional guides). Suspended folders usually have a neat appearance and permit easy storage and removal of records.

Filing Accessories

Folder, guide, and drawer labels may be purchased in several styles. One of the most popular is the self-adhesive type, which requires no moistening.

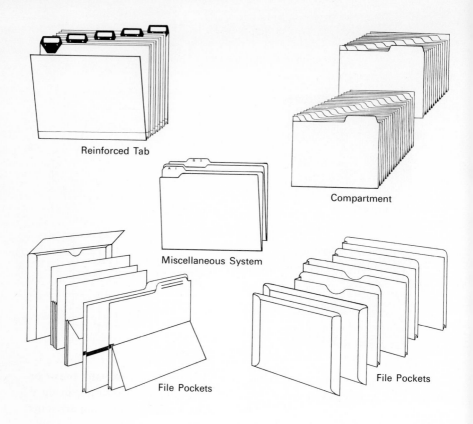

Reinforced Tab

Compartment

Miscellaneous System

File Pockets

File Pockets

Several of the Folders Available for Special Needs

Labels can be bought printed or blank, in strips or rolls, with colors or plain.

Colored signals are useful and can be positioned along the top edges of folders and guides for classification purposes. Signals are also used frequently with visible equipment. They can be fixed or movable and are constructed of paper, plastic, or metal.

Standard printed forms, such as cross-reference sheets, are often made to order for customers by the filing equipment companies. Some companies will print easy-to-read captions on individual folder tabs from a list of names submitted by the customer.

Other equipment that will add to filing efficiency includes the following: file stools to make working at lower drawers comfortable, movable shelves to allow workers to use both hands while filing, drawer dividers to separate records conveniently, sorting devices to speed the preliminary arranging of records, and several types of date stamps, trays, and stands.

For help in selecting equipment and supplies, it is a good idea to have a filing catalog handy for reference. For comparison purposes, two or more

Special Supplies for Housing Punched Tapes and Punched Cards

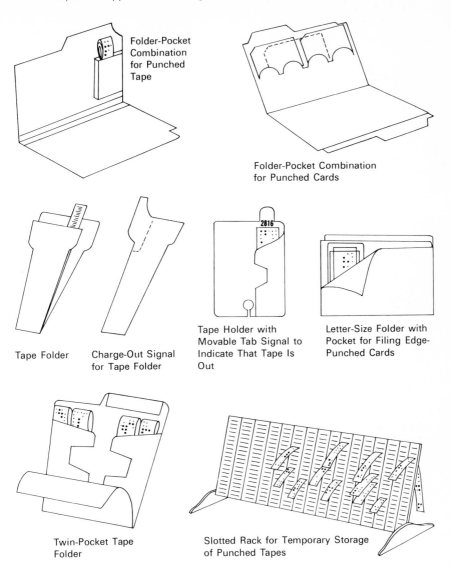

Folder-Pocket Combination for Punched Tape

Folder-Pocket Combination for Punched Cards

Tape Folder

Charge-Out Signal for Tape Folder

Tape Holder with Movable Tab Signal to Indicate That Tape Is Out

Letter-Size Folder with Pocket for Filing Edge-Punched Cards

Twin-Pocket Tape Folder

Slotted Rack for Temporary Storage of Punched Tapes

filing equipment companies should be consulted whenever a large purchase is to be made. These companies have the experience and desire to be helpful not only in providing equipment and supplies but also in helping to design a filing system that will bring top efficiency and satisfaction. The quality of this advisory service is an important factor to consider when deciding from what dealer to buy equipment and supplies.

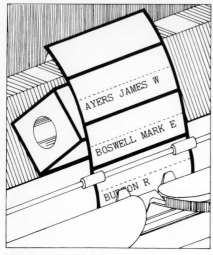

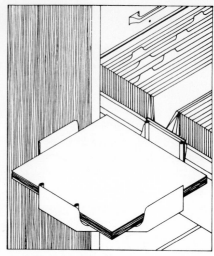

These self-adhesive folder labels are packaged in a special box from which labels can be fed into a typewriter.

The file shelf permits the worker to use both hands while filing.

Cards

The selection of cards to be purchased for both vertical and visible card files is generally the job of the file and records worker or supervisor. "What will the card be used for?" is the key question that should be answered first, not "How much do the cards cost?" The cost of the most expensive cards available is a small fraction of the cost of maintaining them as records. Once their use has been determined, the characteristics of the card needed will depend on:

1. Whether the card will be kept as a permanent or as a temporary record.
2. Whether the record will be handled frequently or infrequently.
3. Whether the card will have a transparent covering for protection or be unprotected.
4. Whether the card will be used for posting (by hand or machine) or for an index.
5. Whether or not the card will be used for classifying items by its color.

A card record that will be kept permanently, handled frequently, or be unprotected should, of course, be heavy and of very high quality. Inexpensive, lighter weight cards may be purchased for temporary, seldom handled, or protected card records. Various weights of file cards are available—light, medium, heavy, and extra-heavy. Various proportions of sulphite and fiber content determine the durability of the cards. A card with a high fiber content is more durable (and more expensive) than a card with a high sulphite content. For posted card records, the relative smoothness of the surface of a card, known as its *finish*, is important. Several finishes are available, from rough to very smooth and glossy, which are best suited to hand and machine posting, respectively.

Card records are sometimes protected by transparent plastic coverings from soiling, bending, and deteriorating. In many visible files the visible edge of the card, because it is most frequently handled, is protected by a clear plastic strip. In vertical card files, cards that are often referred to are sometimes enclosed entirely in cellophane. A device being used in business for permanently enclosing records in clear plastic is the *laminating machine*. A record is fed into the machine, and a plastic coating seals both sides of the record.

In order to classify certain categories in a card file, such as local and out-of-town customers, cards of various colors are often used—perhaps green cards for local customers and blue cards for out-of-town customers. Not only are dozens of solid colors available, but cards may also be purchased with vertical or horizontal stripes. Items are classified according to the color, width, and position of the colored stripes on the cards.

Questions and Problems

1. What sources of information are available about the latest developments in filing equipment and supplies?
2. Substantiate the statement: "Equipment or supplies with any feature that significantly increases the production and efficiency of the worker is probably worthy of purchase."
3. Substantiate the statement: "Equipment or supplies with any feature that will improve protection of records is probably worthy of purchase."
4. What feature will make it easier to open a file drawer?
5. What is the purpose of a file-drawer follower, and what characteristics should it have?
6. Why should guides be *anchored*, and how is this accomplished?
7. Why is work space in a file drawer desirable?
8. What types of file cabinets are available to give work space without loss of filing space?
9. What is the purpose of the correspondence filing space chart on page 132?
10. Enumerate several kinds of special filing cabinets.
11. What are drawer dividers?
12. For what purposes are the file cabinets of various heights used?
13. How do transfer cabinets differ from regular file cabinets?
14. What determines what type of card and visible filing equipment should be used?
15. In what materials are guides available, and what determines the material to be used?

16. What is the purpose of the scores on the front flap of a folder?
17. What are the advantages of a hanging folder?
18. Enumerate the different types of filing labels available.
19. What are *signals,* and for what are they used?
20. What is the advantage of using a filing stool? a filing shelf?
21. What is a good practice to follow whenever a large purchase of filing equipment or supplies is to be made?
22. What factors should determine the quality of a card for office use?
23. How can card records be protected?
24. Describe how color may be used for classification in card systems.

Case Problems in Records Management

1. The McDowell Corporation needs additional file cabinets. Because of a limited budget, the office manager favors the purchase of new economy-grade equipment, which, although attractive in appearance and reinforced at points of wear, does not have drawers with telescoping slides or bearings for easy opening and closing. The file supervisor suggests the purchase of second-hand equipment that does have the drawer slides and bearings and which is available at the same cost as the new equipment. Who do you think is right?

2. The head accountant of Melton Brothers, a large jewelry store with thousands of credit customers, wants to replace the present nonfireproof customer account cabinets with fireproof ones. The general manager has vetoed the request because the present equipment is still in good condition. He further states that when new equipment is to be purchased, the expenditure of $320 for each four-drawer fireproof cabinet as compared with $130 for an ordinary four-drawer file is unnecessary because the store and office building are fireproof. Do you agree with the general manager?

3. Although records are transferred as often as feasible, the active files of the Dawson Company are too crowded for efficient use. Additional floor space is not available for file cabinets. The lease on the present quarters still has three years to run. How would you provide more file space?

4. Carl Porter mentions to his employer, the owner of a travel bureau, that there must be a faster and more efficient way of getting folders and other information for people making personal inquiries. At present he has to walk to the files and storage cabinets in the rear of the office. What would you suggest?

5. Paul Smith has to make frequent use of a large card file. He refers to it to obtain information that requires very little writing. What would you suggest to eliminate the need for his removing the card from the drawer, walking to a desk to record the information, and then returning to reinsert the card in the file?

6. Quite often entire folders must be taken from the files of the Maxson Company and used for extended periods of time. As a result, a considerable number of papers become lost. What would you suggest to reduce this loss?

7. The credit manager of the Daley Company wants the ledger cards of all customers owing money longer than ninety days stored in a tray separate from those of other customers. The accounting clerks protest that this would complicate their work—that when they need information from a customer's card, they would not know in which tray to find it. What is the credit manager's motive, and how would you solve this situation?

8. Miss Kelly, the file supervisor of the Hamilton Corporation, is investigating the purchase of equipment for a new branch office. She estimates that 1,080 inches of records will be filed in the first year of operation.

   Cabinet A has more working space per drawer because of a hinged back that tilts automatically when the drawer is opened. Otherwise, Cabinet A and Cabinet B have identical features. Use the following information to determine how many cabinets would be needed, and what type she should recommend:

   Cabinet A—usable space in each drawer after allowance for working space has been made, 27 inches; cost, four-drawer $130, five-drawer $145.

   Cabinet B—usable space in each drawer after allowance for working space has been made, 24 inches; cost, four-drawer $110, five-drawer $135.

Records Control and Retention

RECORDS CONTROL AND RETENTION refers to the procedures that are used to keep track of business records after they have been created or received and to transfer or dispose of records when they are no longer a part of the day-to-day operations of the organization. With adequate procedures for the control and retention of records, office operations are likely to run smoothly and efficiently. Without such procedures the business runs the risk of losing valuable time and money in its attempt to find records when they are needed for the operation of business systems. In too many business offices, records are filed and forgotten. Principles of control and retention assume that no filed record should be forgotten, that every filed record is of value to the business, and that if a record ceases to be of value to the business, it should be disposed of.

Control of Business Records

File workers may be asked a dozen questions a day about the location of records: "Who borrowed Daniel Jacobs' letter of December 2 from the files?" "When will the November sales summary be returned?" "Has invoice K-2790 shown up?" "May I borrow the November 30 inventory as soon as it is returned?" "How long has Mr. Turner had the Cassel Company folder?" Office employees must not only file the records but also keep track of them as they are being used.

144

The control of records begins even before they are filed (the date-stamp is a means of control) and ends only when the records are disposed of. Because the files themselves organize and thus help control records, papers should be stored as soon as possible after they have been received.

One of the principal problems in control is avoiding the loss of records that are borrowed from the files. A good *charge system* (discussed below) is the best solution. Another problem of controlling records is to prevent them from becoming lost within the files. One of the best precautions against this kind of loss is to follow correct filing procedures and to cross-reference whenever necessary.

A Workable Charge System

"A record that is not worth charging out is not worth filing in the first place" should be the slogan of every file worker. It takes less than thirty seconds to properly charge or sign out a record to a borrower; it may take several hours to find a record that has not been charged. A charge system ensures that all records are accounted for whether they are in the files or in use. Such a system, whether for a large or a small organization, indicates what records are out of the files, who has them, when they were borrowed, and when they will be returned. A file worker performs three jobs in operating a charge system:

1. He handles requests for filed records.
2. He charges the records out.
3. He follows up borrowed records.

The size of the organization will determine the amount of clerical detail that is performed in these jobs. Obviously the charge system will be more formal in a large organization than in a small one, because in a large organization the requests for records are not always made personally, the records are used by more people, and records are stored in several different places. With the increased use of copying machines, offices are increasingly using the copying technique for the control of records. Rather than charge out the original record to a user, a copy is made and sent to the user, and the original is immediately refiled.

Requests for Records

In a large office, records may be requested in several ways: by telephone, by messenger, or in person. Normally all requests should be in writing on a standard *requisition form*. Oral requests should be recorded immediately on requisition forms by the file workers. The forms may be designed in the office or purchased; in either case, they should provide the following information: (1) name or subject of record, (2) date of record, (3) signature or name of borrower, (4) date borrowed, and (5) date the record is to be followed up to ensure return. Whenever possible, the requisition should be signed by the borrower. (The signature provides definite proof of who has what.) The requisition form may also include the name of the borrower's department and the subject of the record.

In a small office, where requests are usually made personally or where the borrower himself removes the records from the file, the use of a requisition form is unnecessary if the papers are to be returned to the files immediately. However, if the records are not to be returned at once, a form should be filled in because it is the basis for the second procedure in a charge system: charging out the records.

Charging Out Records

When an entire folder is removed from the files, an *out guide* or an *out folder* should be placed in the location of the borrowed folder. When an individual paper is removed from a folder, a *substitution card* should be placed in the folder exactly where the paper was. These charge-out forms indicate who has the record and the date it was removed from the files. Charge forms are useful in three ways: (1) they show that records are being used and have not been lost or misfiled, (2) they enable the file worker to follow up the borrowed records to make sure they get back to the file, and (3) they act as bookmarks to make refiling easy.

Out guides are made of the same heavy cardboard as filing guides. Two popular types that may be obtained are (1) a guide with a pocket at the front for a requisition slip or (2) a cumulative guide, which has a form attached for entering each user's name. Both kinds of out guides have advantages: the pocket type eliminates the need for transferring the information on the

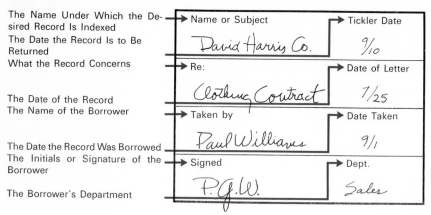

Information Contained on a Requisition

Even though each of these charge-out forms differs in size and makeup, each contains (1) the name, (2) the date of the record, (3) the name of the borrower, (4) the date the record was borrowed, and (5) the date the record is to be returned (follow-up date).

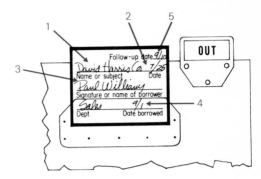

Out Guide with Requisition Card in a Transparent Pocket

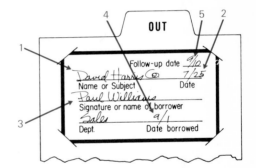

Substitution Card with Requisition Card Attached

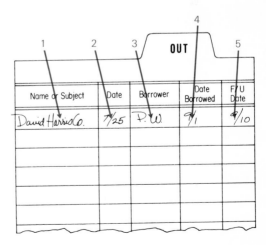

Cumulative Substitution Card

requisition slip; the cumulative type provides a history of how the records have been used and by whom.

Another type of out guide that is used for punched card files is the octagonal flasher card. These cards slip easily into the files and remain with one edge exposed, indicating that a card has been removed. The use of five different colors makes color-control of retrieved cards automatic.

Instead of out guides, many people prefer to use folders. Their advantage is that records can be stored temporarily in them. Thus filing does not have to be delayed until a borrowed folder is returned. The front of an out folder is usually like that of a cumulative out guide.

Many experts recommend that the original folder remain in the drawer and that the contents be transferred to a special *carrier folder*. Carrier folders are made of a heavy material that can withstand extensive handling. Furthermore, they are usually of a distinctive color, which signals their importance. This helps prevent their loss and expedites their return to the files.

As with out guides, substitution cards may be either the pocket type with space for the requisition slip or the cumulative type. These cards are of a special color and are small enough to be inserted in a folder to indicate the absence of a paper.

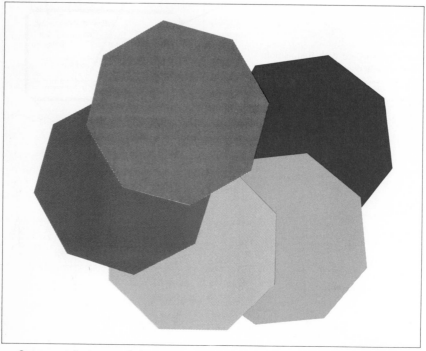

Octagonal flasher cards in various colors are used to signal the removal of a punched card from a file.

In a large organization, records are sometimes requested and then sent in turn to several people or departments. Hours would be wasted if these papers were returned to the file department for recharging and redelivery after each person had finished with them. For efficiency, these two timesaving charge methods are widely used:

1. As each person finishes using the papers, he delivers them to the next person requesting them and fills out a *recharge form*. This form is sent to the file department, which recharges the out guide.

2. A form that lists, in order, all the individuals wanting the record is attached to the record. As the record travels from one individual to another, each initials the form. A duplicate copy of this *routing slip* is kept with the charge-out form so that the record can be traced if necessary.

When papers are returned to the files, the out guide, out folder, or substitution card is removed and the charge-out notation canceled.

Following Up Borrowed Records

The kind of business and the importance of the records will determine how long papers may be borrowed. Some records are so important that they are never taken away from the file area. Confidential or very valuable records usually must be returned to the files every night. Typical records may be kept longer, depending on the period set by the office manager or other

Courtesy Tab Products Company

Out guides are readily visible when inserted in the place of a borrowed folder.

Name	Address	Subject
Miller Tire Supply Co.	Cleveland, Ohio	New Model 2-8A21

Date of Record	Date Taken	Date Returned
5/12/--	5/20/--	

Routing (Place numbers, 1, 2, 3, etc., in boxes to indicate routing)

ACCOUNTING	☐ ____	PERSONNEL	☐ ____	
ADVERTISING	☐ ____	PRODUCTION	2 ____	
MARKETING	☐ ____	STORES	3 ____	
SALES	☐ ____	ADMINISTRATION	☐ ____	
PURCHASING	1 HD	RETURN TO FILES	4 ____	

This routing form shows that the record to which it is attached has been sent to the purchasing department (initials) and will be sent to the production and stores departments before being returned to the files.

executives. In any event, a schedule should be set up for calling for papers that are due. Overdue records should either be recharged or returned immediately. Any experienced office worker will agree that the longer records are out of the files, the greater is their likelihood of being misplaced. Systematic and determined follow-up will reduce possibilities of such loss.

If the organization is small, it is easy for the person responsible for the files to check the out guides, out folders, or substitution cards for the due dates of borrowed records. When the organization is large, however, many file drawers would have to be checked. Therefore, the follow-up job must be simplified, usually by the use of a card follow-up, or *tickler file*, system. In the latter system, when records are requested, a duplicate copy of the requisition form is placed in a separate tickler file behind the date on which the borrowed records are due. The tickler can then be checked very quickly every day. The original copy of the requisition form is placed on the out guide, out folder, or substitution card in the main file.

Sometimes the file department receives a requisition form for records to be delivered at some future date. Such requisitions can be filed under that date in a tickler file. It is a good idea to have separate tickler files for follow-up and for advance requests, although one tickler could be used for both purposes.

Even with a good charge system, papers are occasionally lost. If an organized search for the papers does not succeed, the original information should be listed from memory or other sources on a colored sheet and stored in place

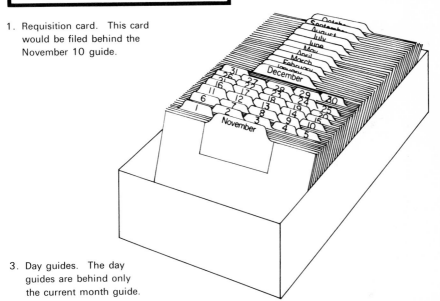

Name or Subject	Tickler Date
David Harris Co.	11/10
Re:	Date of letter
Clothing contract	9/12
Taken by	Date taken
PAUL WILLIAMS	11/1
Signed	Dept.
P.G.W.	Sales

A Tickler File
for the Follow-Up
of Borrowed Records

1. Requisition card. This card would be filed behind the November 10 guide.

2. Month guides. The current month guide is always in front.

3. Day guides. The day guides are behind only the current month guide.

of the lost record. This procedure will ensure that no one will waste his time searching for lost records.

A charge system will function properly only when everyone follows the charge procedures adopted. If persons other than file workers have access to the files, these persons (including executives) should be required to charge to themselves all records they remove.

Follow-Up Files as Reminders

Incoming and outgoing correspondence frequently must be acted upon at some future date. For example, sending a customer a price list he has requested may have to wait until new price lists are delivered from the printer.

How to Conduct an Organized Search for a Lost Record

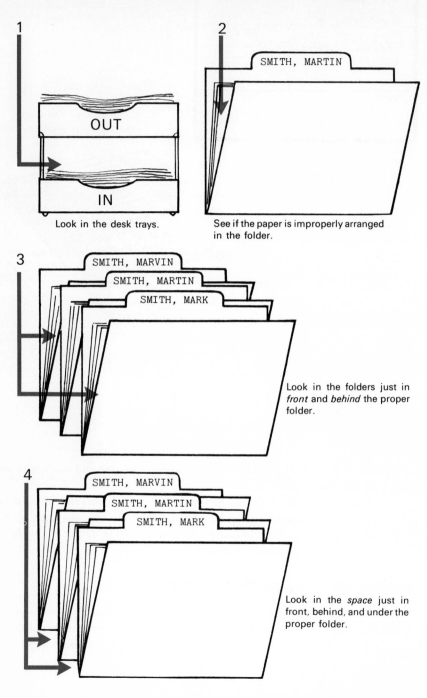

1 Look in the desk trays.

2 See if the paper is improperly arranged in the folder.

3 Look in the folders just in *front* and *behind* the proper folder.

4 Look in the *space* just in front, behind, and under the proper folder.

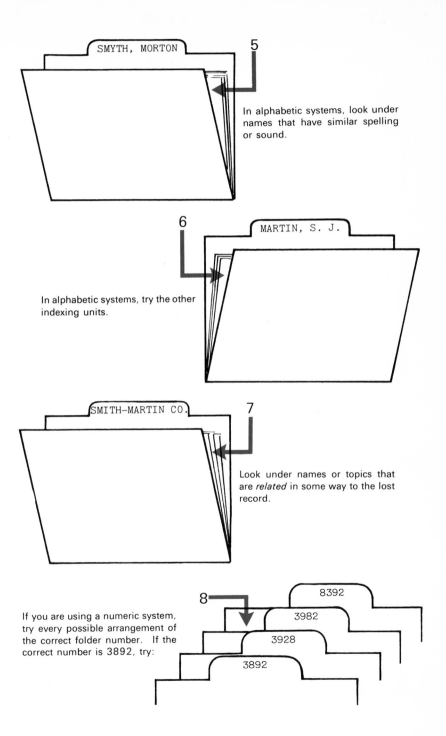

SMYTH, MORTON   5

In alphabetic systems, look under names that have similar spelling or sound.

6   **MARTIN, S. J.**

In alphabetic systems, try the other indexing units.

SMITH—MARTIN CO.   7

Look under names or topics that are *related* in some way to the lost record.

If you are using a numeric system, try every possible arrangement of the correct folder number. If the correct number is 3892, try:

8

8392

3982

3928

3892

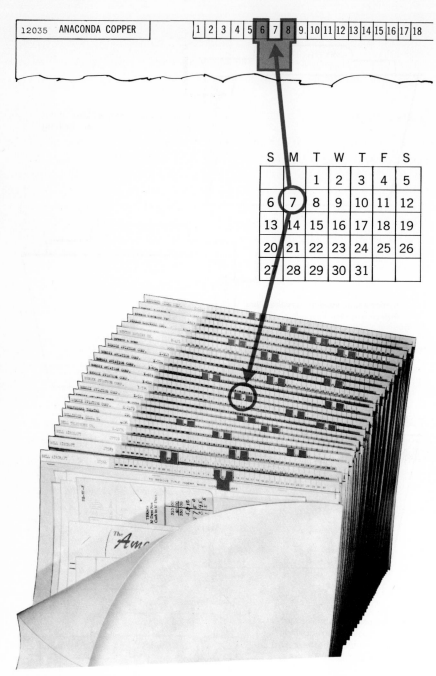

The figure on this follow-up folder indicates that the seventh of the current month is the follow-up date.

Special follow-up folders can be used to house such correspondence temporarily. A movable signal at the top edge of the folder indicates the date its contents must be acted upon. Other office reminders are desk calendars, tickler files, and combination alphabetic and date files.

Transfer and Disposal of Business Records

The final steps in the life cycle of a record are transfer and disposal. The regular transfer of inactive records results in economy of space, equipment, and labor by reducing the office space needed for active files, making possible the use of inexpensive equipment and supplies for the transferred records, and streamlining the active files, so that records can be found with utmost efficiency. How a program of transfer and disposal operates depends upon the answers to these questions: How valuable are the records compared with the cost of keeping them? How often are they used? When can they be destroyed without risking undue loss or inconvenience?

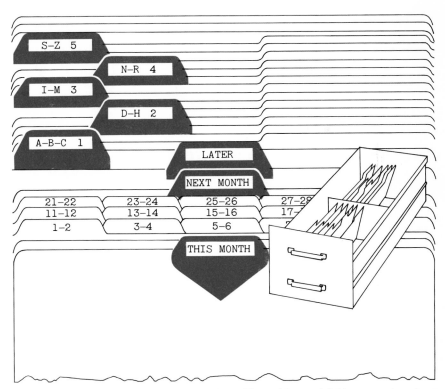

A combination alphabetic and date file. The guides and folders are placed sideways in a desk drawer.

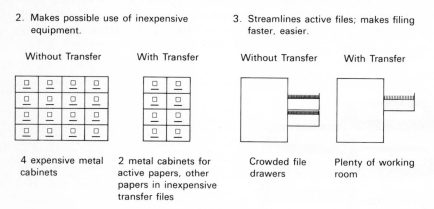

1. Reduces amount of valuable floor space needed.

Without Transfer　　　With Transfer

How Planned Transfer of Records Saves Time and Money

4 filing cabinets　　　2 filing cabinets, desk in same space

2. Makes possible use of inexpensive equipment.

Without Transfer　　　With Transfer

4 expensive metal cabinets　　　2 metal cabinets for active papers, other papers in inexpensive transfer files

3. Streamlines active files; makes filing faster, easier.

Without Transfer　　　With Transfer

Crowded file drawers　　　Plenty of working room

How Businesses Value Records

In determining the value of their records, many businesses analyze and classify them as follows:

1. *Vital records.* These include legal papers of incorporation, titles to ownership, deeds, major contracts, property plans, reports to stockholders, minutes of directors' meetings, and insurance policies. They should never be destroyed because they are essential to the existence of the organization and are often irreplaceable.

2. *Important records.* These include invoices, accounts receivable, sales records, quotations, financial statements, and certain correspondence. They facilitate the routine of the business and are replaceable only at great cost and with much delay. They may be transferred to inactive storage space if they are not being used and placed in containers that will keep them in good condition.

3. *Useful records.* These include some general correspondence, memorandums, and bank statements. They are temporarily helpful and are replaceable

at slight cost. They are often destroyed from a few weeks to a year after they are received.

4. *Nonessential papers.* These include routine inquiries, announcements, and acknowledgments. They should never be filed with more important records, and they may be destroyed after temporary use.

Once the value of records has been determined, it is necessary to decide upon the length of time to keep them, or the *retention period.* The nature of the business, the type of papers handled, the information derived from them, and the law are several factors that will influence this decision.

The following suggested retention schedule is presented as an example of one that might be adopted for a particular business.[1]

PERMANENT RECORDS

Appropriation ledger, authorizations, and end-of-year trial balances
Audit reports of CPAs
Canceled checks for important payments, i.e., taxes, purchases of property, special contracts, etc. (checks should be filed with the papers pertaining to the underlying transaction)
Capital stock and bond records: ledgers, transfer registers, stubs showing issues, record of interest coupons, options, etc.
Cash books
Chart of accounts
Correspondence (legal and important matters only)
Deeds, mortgages, and bills of sale, as well as contracts and leases still in effect
Depreciation schedules
Financial statements—end of year (other time periods optional)
General and private ledgers and end-of-year trial balances
Insurance records, current accident reports, claims, policies, etc.
Journals
Minute books of directors and stockholders, including by-laws and charter
Property appraisals by outside appraisers
Property records—including costs, depreciation reserves, and end-of-year trial balances, depreciation schedules, blueprints and plans
Tax returns and worksheets, revenue agents' reports, and other documents relating to determination of income tax liability
Trademark registrations

SIX TO SEVEN YEARS

Accident reports and claims (settled cases)
Accounts payable
Accounts receivable ledgers and trial balances
Canceled checks
Canceled stock and bond certificates and expired options
Contracts and leases (expired)
Expense analyses and expense distribution schedules
Inventories of products, materials, and supplies
Invoices to customers

[1] Arnold C. Soney, "How Long Should a Business Keep Records?" *The Practical Accountant,* I, September-October, 1968, p. 18.

Invoices from vendors (see Vouchers below)
Notes receivable ledgers and trial balances
Payroll records and summaries, including payments to pensioners
Plant cost ledgers
Purchase orders (purchasing department copy)
Sales records
Scrap and salvage records—inventories, sales, etc.
Subsidiary ledgers to the general ledger and trial balances
Time books
Voucher register and trial balances
Vouchers for payments to vendors, employees, etc. (includes allowances and reimbursement of employees, officers, etc., for travel and entertainment expenses)

TWO TO THREE YEARS

Applications for employment
General correspondence
Insurance policies that have expired
Internal audit reports, including working papers (in some situations, longer retention periods may be desirable)
Miscellaneous internal reports
Petty cash vouchers
Physical inventory tags
Savings bond registration records of employees

ONE YEAR OR LESSER PERIOD

Bank reconciliations (keep one year)
Bank statements (after reconciliation and audit)
Correspondence of an unimportant nature with customers or vendors
Duplicate deposit slips
Purchase orders (except purchasing department copy)
Receiving sheets
Requisitions
Stenographers' notebooks
Stockroom withdrawal forms
Tabulating cards

Plans of Transfer

There are several plans for the transfer of records. The one selected will depend on the nature and frequency of reference, the space available, and the filing system in use. In general, transfer plans are basically either *periodic* or *perpetual*.

Periodic Transfer

Periodic transfer is the removal of papers at the end of a definite *filing period* (at the end of each year, for example) from the active files to inexpensive transfer files. Periodic transfer can be operated in at least three ways: one period, two period, or maximum-minimum period.

In the one-period plan, only the papers for the current filing period occupy the active files. On certain dates the folders and their contents are moved directly to the transfer files and a new filing period is started. Even though this transfer plan is easy to operate, it has a definite disadvantage. For a while, frequent trips will have to be made to the transfer files to consult records from the previous filing period. If the transfer files are located away from the office, much valuable time may be lost.

In the two-period plan, the files are divided to provide space for two filing periods—the present period and the period immediately preceding. Records of the present period are referred to as *active;* those of the previous period are called *inactive.* At the end of each filing period, the following changes

Periodic Plans for Transferring Records

A-B ACTIVE	**M-N** ACTIVE
C-E ACTIVE	**O-R** ACTIVE
F-H ACTIVE	**S-T** ACTIVE
I-L ACTIVE	**U-Z** ACTIVE

With the one-period plan, all file drawers are active.

With the two-period plan and five-drawer files, inactive files often may be contracted to fit the top and the bottom drawers.

A-E INACTIVE	**I-Q** INACTIVE
A-B ACTIVE	**M-N** ACTIVE
C-F ACTIVE	**O-S** ACTIVE
G-L ACTIVE	**T-Z** ACTIVE
F-H INACTIVE	**R-Z** INACTIVE

A-E ACTIVE	**L-R** ACTIVE
F-K ACTIVE	**S-Z** ACTIVE
A-E INACTIVE	**L-R** INACTIVE
F-K INACTIVE	**S-Z** INACTIVE

With the two-period plan and four-drawer files, the upper two rows hold active papers, and the lower two rows hold inactive records.

In this two-period plan, the active files stand beside the inactive.

A-B ACTIVE	**A-B** INACTIVE	**K-L** ACTIVE	**K-L** INACTIVE
C ACTIVE	**C** INACTIVE	**M-N** ACTIVE	**M-N** INACTIVE
D-E ACTIVE	**D-E** INACTIVE	**O-R** ACTIVE	**O-R** INACTIVE
F-G ACTIVE	**F-G** INACTIVE	**S** ACTIVE	**S** INACTIVE
H-J ACTIVE	**H-J** INACTIVE	**T-Z** ACTIVE	**T-Z** INACTIVE

take place: (1) the inactive records are removed to transfer files, (2) the active records become inactive and are placed in the inactive drawers, and (3) the active drawers are now empty, ready to receive records for the next filing period. This plan eliminates the disadvantage of the one-period plan because only the oldest papers have been removed to transfer files, and the current records and the records of the previous period are still readily available. With a two-period plan, the fatigue that comes from working in a stooped or tip-toe position can be reduced by reserving easily-accessible file drawers for active records.

An adaptation of the two-period plan to eliminate switching records from active to inactive file drawers at the end of a filing period operates as follows: An active cabinet stands beside an inactive one. At the end of a filing period, the records in the active cabinet automatically become inactive, and they are not moved. The records in the inactive cabinet are transferred, leaving this cabinet empty—ready for new records. Then, simply by interchanging "active" and "inactive" drawer labels, the file worker readies the two cabinets for the next period.

In the maximum-minimum period plan, the least recent papers are moved directly from the active files to the transfer files at the end of each filing period. Inactive files are not used. However, because the most recent records are kept in the active files, the disadvantage of the one-period plan is overcome. To use this plan, a business must establish maximum and minimum periods of time for keeping records in the active files.

Perpetual Transfer

Under the perpetual plan, papers are transferred from the active files constantly, or *perpetually*. This plan is generally used when the nature of a business makes it difficult to set definite filing periods. For example, in the type of work done by building contractors, architects, or lawyers, the length of time taken to complete the work varies with each job or case. Transferring records on a periodic basis might result, therefore, in the removal of frequently used records. Under the perpetual transfer plan, whenever a job or case is completed, all records pertaining to it are moved from the active files to the inactive or transfer files.

Transfer Equipment and Supplies

Other than items mentioned in Chapter 9, transfer equipment and supplies include (1) card files that indicate the contents of transfer files and the destruction dates of the papers; (2) transfer file accessories, such as labels, drawer dividers, metal clips to connect file units, drawer locks, and removable blocks; and (3) special transfer files for cards, microfilms, invoices, and other records

How the Maximum-Minimum Transfer Plan Operates

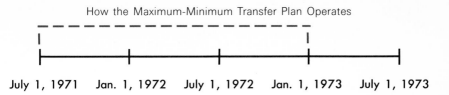

July 1, 1971   Jan. 1, 1972   July 1, 1972   Jan. 1, 1973   July 1, 1973

1. On January 1, 1973, files contain records from as early as July 1, 1971, or eighteen months old (maximum period).

TRANSFERRED

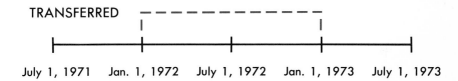

July 1, 1971   Jan. 1, 1972   July 1, 1972   Jan. 1, 1973   July 1, 1973

2. On the same day, January 1, 1973, records of the earliest six months are transferred, leaving records of the last twelve months (minimum period).

TRANSFERRED

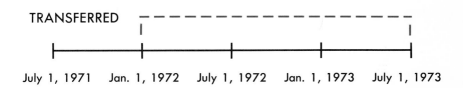

July 1, 1971   Jan. 1, 1972   July 1, 1972   Jan. 1, 1973   July 1, 1973

3. Six months later, July 1, 1973, the files have accumulated the records of the past eighteen months (maximum period).

TRANSFERRED   TRANSFERRED

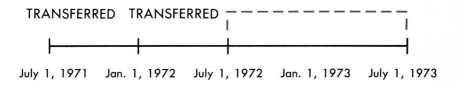

July 1, 1971   Jan. 1, 1972   July 1, 1972   Jan. 1, 1973   July 1, 1973

4. On the same day, July 1, 1973, records of the earliest six months are transferred, again leaving records of the last twelve months (minimum period).

of various sizes. Open-shelf, interlocking transfer file units are also available for the storage of punched cards.

When records are transferred, the guides are usually left in the active files and the old miscellaneous folders are moved in front of the individual folders in the transfer files to serve as guides. Transfer files do not normally provide for guides with rod extensions.

Getting Ready for Transfer

The work of transferal can be made easier and can be speeded up by combining a part of it with another filing operation. Ordinarily at transfer time, before the records can be physically transferred or destroyed, a decision must be made as to what should be kept for how long. Arriving at that decision is the most difficult part of the transfer operation and is a big responsibility for a file worker. Many organizations, however, make this

Steps in Planning Transfer

1. Prepare a list of correspondents that will need new folders.

2. Type labels for the new folders; prepare the folders.

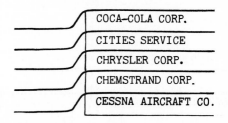

3. Assemble transfer boxes and label them.

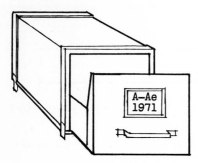

4. Discard previously transferred papers that are no longer needed. Authority should be in writing.

decision at the time the record is first released for filing. Instead of simply initialing in the upper left corner to give authority to file, the receiver of the record releases it by indicating in the upper left corner how long it should be kept in the active file and whether or not after that period it should be transferred or destroyed. Releasing records for the files in this manner not only puts the decision on the person best qualified to make it but also speeds up the actual transfer operation.

By performing the following activities a week or two ahead of time, the file worker will make the transfer job easier. Interference with the regular use of the files will also be reduced.

1. The file worker should prepare new folders for the active files.

2. He should make sure that transfer files or boxes are available. The file worker should attach labels to show clearly what the contents will be and what the inclusive dates will be.

3. He should remove from the old transfer files papers no longer of value and dispose of them. No papers should be disposed of without authority, preferably in writing.

A Pressboard Transfer File

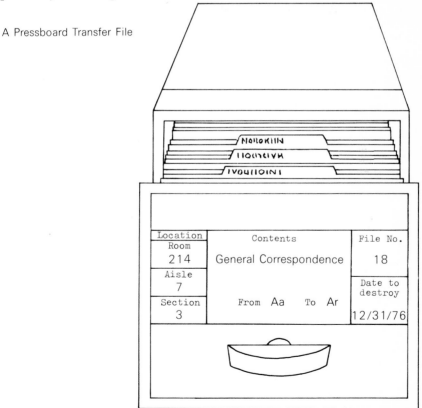

Methods of Disposal

Some records are destroyed by being fed through a specially designed shredding machine, which cuts them into narrow strips. Other methods of disposal are burning the records, selling them for scrap, or simply throwing them away. The confidential nature and the quantity of papers will usually determine the manner of disposal.

Microfilming

A filing technique that is used in many offices for both transferal and current record storage is *microfilming*, a process of making miniature copies of records on film and storing the film in small reels or strips. Thus the original bulky records may be destroyed and the films can be filed in only a small fraction of the space that would be needed to store the original records. When required, the records can be viewed on a machine that shows them enlarged to approximately their original size.

Almost all transferred papers and many inactive or semiactive ones lend themselves to storage on film. For such records microfilming has the following advantages:

Courtesy The Paige Co., Inc.

These records of a large corporation have been transferred to basement storage space.

1. Approximately 98 percent of conventional filing space is saved. This is probably the greatest advantage of microfilming.

2. Costs of file cabinets and equipment are cut. One microfilm cabinet will store on film the contents of about 160 four-drawer correspondence files.

3. Records can be kept in the main office area for reference and do not have to be moved to inconvenient storage rooms.

4. Any one record on a reel of film is in permanent sequence and cannot become disarranged or lost.

5. Large numbers of valuable microfilmed records can easily be stored in relatively small fire-resistant containers for protection against fire, theft, or other loss.

6. The labor costs of handling and maintaining large quantities of records are lower when they are on microfilm.

7. Microfilmed records are durable and are generally acceptable as legal evidence in courts of law.

Banks use microfilming to obtain copies of canceled checks; department stores, dairies, and bus companies, for billing operations; railroads, for freight waybill handling; and publishers, for subscription work. In other words, microphotography is not only a filing technique but also a means of carrying on the everyday operations of business.

The Microfilming Operation

The sequence of events in the microfilming operation will depend on the needs of the organization. An example of one such operation is illustrated on page 166. All microfilming operations, however, include the following basic steps:

1. *The records are photographed,* usually on 100-foot reels of 16mm film, by means of a *microfilmer.* A 100-foot reel of film will photograph 13,000 bank checks, or 5,800 6- by 4-inch cards, or 3,000 letters. Several types of microfilmers are available. One requires manual feeding of papers into the machine; another has automatic feed; some types can be fitted with devices to endorse or cancel checks while they photograph. Papers can be fed into the machines at the rate of 185 to 500 a minute, depending on the type of document. The machines have automatic safeguards to prevent two papers from being fed in simultaneously. It is important that records be in correct sequence before they are microfilmed, because the sequence of filmed records cannot be changed.

2. *The filmed records are indexed.* Special index signals, such as flash cards or reference lines, are photographed on the same rolls of microfilm as the documents. These signals speed up reference to photographed records when the film is being viewed. Reels of film are stored in boxes, which must also be labeled for filing. The outside of the film box indicates the contents of

A Typical Microfilming Operation

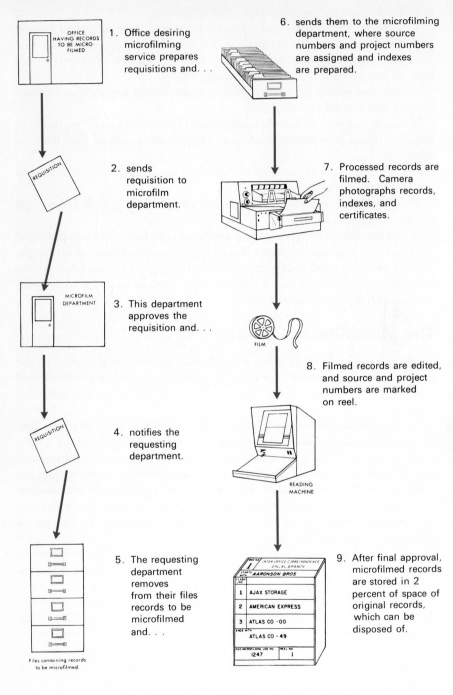

1. Office desiring microfilming service prepares requisitions and. . .

2. sends requisition to microfilm department.

3. This department approves the requisition and. . .

4. notifies the requesting department.

5. The requesting department removes from their files records to be microfilmed and. . .

6. sends them to the microfilming department, where source numbers and project numbers are assigned and indexes are prepared.

7. Processed records are filmed. Camera photographs records, indexes, and certificates.

8. Filmed records are edited, and source and project numbers are marked on reel.

9. After final approval, microfilmed records are stored in 2 percent of space of original records, which can be disposed of.

Files containing records to be microfilmed.

A Microfilmer

the reel. The film file drawer, which houses many of these boxes, is also labeled to indicate what boxes it contains.

3. *The films are viewed* on a type of projector, known as a *reader,* that can be operated manually or electrically. It enlarges the documents for easy reading; some models are equipped to make full-size copies of filmed records.

4. *Boxes of microfilm are filed* in specially designed file cabinets.

When to Microfilm

The cost of microfilming is estimated to be about $20 to $30 for each drawer of files to be photographed. Since reference to film is not usually as easy as reference to papers, the volume of records and the frequency of reference made to them before and after transfer must be considered in deciding when to microfilm. The following general statements are guides in making this decision.

1. When records are very valuable and irreplaceable, it is economical to

Courtesy Eastman Kodak

A Microfilm Reader

microfilm them immediately. The film copy should be stored in a safe location away from the original record—an application of the saying, "Don't put all your eggs in one basket." For double protection, some microfilming machines can take two identical rolls of pictures simultaneously. One roll can be used currently, and one can be for branch-office use or vault storage.

2. When records are to be retained less than seven years, it is usually less costly to transfer them to storage areas than to microfilm them.

3. When records are to be retained from seven to twelve years, they are good microfilming possibilities. The comparative costs of storing full-sized papers and microfilming should be studied.

4. When records are to be retained longer than twelve years, it is usually more economical to microfilm them than to store the original records.

Microfiche

Microfiche (pronounced micro-feesh) is miniature photographic reproduction on cards rather than strips of film. A standard microfiche card, measuring 6 by 4 inches, will photograph 60 or more pages of records. Two microfiche file drawers, which occupy about the same space as one standard vertical file drawer, will store the images of about 240,000 records. Because microfiche images are smaller than microfilm images and because the cards are filed

A Microfiche Card

vertically with no wasted space, microfiche takes even less storage space per record than microfilm. Microfiche cards are viewed on a machine that is similar in design to the microfilm reader.

An advantage of microfiche over microfilm is that small groups of microfiche records (one or more cards) can be removed from the file without disturbing other records. This is usually not possible with microfilm because records are photographed on long reels of film. Hence microfiche is a medium of communications in that miniature records can be sent from one location to another very easily and at great postage savings. The federal government accepts microfiche records in place of voluminous reports and tax records. Lengthy catalogs and reference books are frequently sent from one branch office to another on microfiche. Machines that will print full-size copies of the photographed records in seconds are available for both microfilm and microfiche. The future promises even further miniaturization of records. One new process reduces 3,200 business documents to a single 6- by 4-inch transparency.

Questions and Problems

1. What is one of the best assurances against losses within the files?
2. What are the jobs one does in operating a charge system?
3. Why should a requisition form be signed by the borrower? What other information should it contain?

4. What is the purpose of out guides? out folders? substitution cards?
5. Why is the out folder preferred by many people?
6. What is a carrier folder, and how is it used?
7. How may charged papers be transferred to another person without returning them to the files?
8. What should a file worker do as soon as records have been returned to the files?
9. What should be done when a record cannot be found?
10. What types of files can be used as reminder systems?
11. What are the four classifications of records according to their value?
12. What is the name given to the period of time records are kept? What factors will influence the length of this period?
13. What are the two general plans of transfer?
14. What is the principal disadvantage of the one-period transfer plan?
15. Explain the two-period transfer plan.
16. How does the maximum-minimum transfer plan operate?
17. Under what conditions is it wise to use the perpetual transfer method?
18. What activities can be performed in advance to facilitate transfer?
19. What is microfilming, and what is its major advantage?
20. Give several comparisons of the space requirements of filing full-size papers and filing microfilms.
21. Describe some of the features of a microfilmer.
22. How is microfilm read?
23. Name an application of microfilming other than the filing function.
24. What is microfiche?
25. Name the advantages of microfiche over microfilm.

Case Problems in Records Management

1. Mr. Lynch, the office manager for an organization with 100 office workers, has decided to dispense with requisition slips, substitution cards, out folders and guides, and any system of charge-out. The only means of follow-up that will be in effect will be the establishment of a rule requiring that all records borrowed from the files be returned between 4:30 and 5 every Friday afternoon. What advantages do you think he sees in such a plan? Do you agree? If you have any objections, state them.
2. The filing department supervisor has suggested to the office manager that all requisition slips be submitted in duplicate. Why do you think she wants the second copy?
3. The office manager is considering the adoption of a procedure whereby an entire folder would be sent to a borrower, even though only one or a few records were requested from that folder. What are the advantages and disadvantages of such a procedure?

4. Design a routing form for use when the same records are to be sent to a number of individuals before the records are returned to files.

5. Because Mr. Barnes and his secretary are the only people working in a small travel bureau, he has decided it is not worth the time to transfer records. He is going to keep all records, current and noncurrent, in the same files. Do you think this is advisable?

6. Miss Lacey has decided to spread the transfer of records over a period of six months by transferring the *A* through *D* records during one month, the *E* through *H* records the next month, and so on through the various divisions of the alphabet. At the end of six months, when the entire alphabet has been completed, she will then start through it again. Would you use such a system? Why?

7. The XYZ Corporation has 12 four-drawer, letter-size files which occupy a total of 72 square feet of office space. The contents of 6 of these files are transferred every year to inexpensive four-drawer transfer cases that are housed in the basement of the building. The XYZ Corporation is paying 20 cents a square foot a month for its office space and 5 cents a square foot a month for the basement space. The regular filing cabinets cost $97 each, and the transfer cases cost $12 each. How much money does the corporation save each year by transferring its records? What other saving is effected by the transfer?

8. When you wish to know a telephone number and do not have a directory, you call "Information," and the operator obtains the number for you from the proper telephone book. The number of directories from which an information operator must work is considerable. In New York City, for example, each information operator has about 15,000 pages with over 5 million listings, or the equivalent of one directory 3 feet thick! Can you suggest a faster, less cumbersome, space-saving way of listing the names and telephone numbers for these information operators?

Creating
Records Systems

THE COST OF RECORDS MANAGEMENT is high, and it gets higher every day as paper work volume increases. It is imperative, therefore, that an organization make decisions that will create the best records management system for its needs and then keep that system at peak efficiency in terms of logical organization, thoughtful creation of records, and thrifty operation.

For every record a business receives or creates—from a penciled memorandum to a formal contract—the following records management decisions must be carefully made:

1. Should the record be kept?
2. Where should it be stored?
3. How should it be classified? (Alphabetically, numerically, geographically, by subject, by date, or by some combination of these?)
4. What should be the arrangement of the files in which the records are stored?

Should the Record Be Kept?

Surprisingly few of the records a business uses should be kept for any significant length of time. Some companies have made careful studies and found that they were keeping far too many records. For example:

1. More credit buying means more customer records.

2. More budgets, forecasts, and other papers from "scientific management."

3. Government tax and other regulations require complete, accurate records.

4. Temptation with modern equipment to produce more copies than necessary.

Campbell Soup Company found, as a result of an analysis of its records, that 44 percent could be destroyed and 34 percent could be removed to storage centers. Only 22 percent were needed in the active files.

Atlantic Richfield destroyed 39 percent of its records and removed 36 percent to inexpensive storage space. It kept only 25 percent in the active files.

A survey of the records of the State of Illinois led to a saving of about $850,000 a year by stopping the creation of more than 10 million unnecessary pieces of paper annually. At the outset, 480 tons of paper were destroyed!

Of course, the two extremes of keeping all records or throwing all records away are easy, because neither requires decisions. But these extremes are expensive, as illustrated on page 174.

In deciding which records should be kept, certain questions about the organization need to be answered.

What Is the Line of Business? A wholesale electrical dealer, for example, needs an inventory file of the products in stock, whereas an architectural firm needs a blueprint file.

How Is the Business Organized? A cosmetics manufacturer that has a home office and two branch offices might find it necessary to file three copies of the same market survey—one in each office. A one-building clothing manufacturer would probably need to file only one copy of a similar record.

Costs can be lowered by keeping only useful records.

Too Few Records Saved

Too Many Records Saved

$ HIGH COST

High cost because:
1. Important records often are not available.
2. There are few records on which to base good business decisions.

High cost because:
1. Records are hard to find.
2. Labor costs are high.
3. Equipment and maintenance costs are high.

$ LOW COST

Only Useful Records Saved

Low cost because:
1. Records are easy to find.
2. Labor cost is reasonable.
3. Maintenance cost is reasonable.

What Information Do Executives, Managers, and Workers Need? The personnel manager of a manufacturing plant involved in space technology will want to know test scores of applicants for this highly technical work. Consequently, he is likely to keep an employee test-record file. The boss of a heavy construction company does not feel that formal tests for the laborers he hires are necessary in his line of business. Thus he will have no need for a test file. As obvious as the example above sounds, failure to ask, "What information is needed?" for each piece of correspondence is the leading reason for filing inefficiency in most businesses. A letter that was found in the files of a real estate office is reproduced on page 176. This letter had been in the active files for several years; yet none of the office workers could recall ever referring to it, and the office manager admitted that it and others should never have been placed in storage. Because no one has said, "Throw them away," thousands of such letters clutter the files of business.

Incoming correspondence is frequently filed only because an employee predicts that the address will be needed. This practice is usually not justified. If the address is important, it should be transferred to a card file, which can be quickly and easily referred to; then the correspondence can be discarded.

Is Retention of This Record Required by the Government? Some city governments require the local electric power company to keep on file the reports of electrical inspections of homes in the city. A heating gas company might be held responsible for keeping an accurate file of all gas lines and other property. And every business is required to keep complete tax records and many other records for city, state, and federal purposes.

Is There Some Legal Necessity for the Record? The trust department of a bank, for example, keeps many records, such as wills, that are seldom referred to and are not necessarily required by government regulation. However, such records are kept to protect the legal interests of both the bank and its customers. The average person should keep receipts for goods purchased for the same reasons—as supporting proof for a possible claim later.

The answers to these five questions should tell the office worker whether a record should be filed. The answers will also help office managers to set policies as to what types of records should be kept. Without such policies, the average file becomes a catchall for most of the correspondence received and created in an office. Important-looking but worthless papers are often filed, and important but hastily written memorandums are sometimes discarded in offices that do not have a sound records management program. Offices that ask the questions enumerated and form policies based on the answers generally operate with a minimum of confusion and a maximum of efficiency.

Box 1726
Fairborn, Ohio 43432
April 2, 1968

Harris Realty Company
3491 Campbell Avenue
Dayton, Ohio 45414

Gentlemen:

   Would you please send me a copy of the free brochure, "Saving on Household Repairs," that was mentioned in your local newspaper advertisement of March 25.

   Thank you very much.

                    Yours truly,

                    J. Donald Walton
                    J. Donald Walton

This piece of correspondence probably should have been destroyed as soon as the request was filled.

Where Should It Be Stored?

In large businesses having several departments, records are usually located in (1) centralized files, in which certain records for the entire organization are combined and kept in a central file room; (2) departmental files, kept in the offices of separate departments—these files contain only the records for those departments, such as sales or advertising; and (3) a combination of centralized and departmental files. Illustrated on this page are floorplans of centralized and departmental file locations for a business having several departments.

The charts on pages 178 and 179 show when records should be filed centrally and when they should be located in one of the departments of a business.

Some large businesses do not have centralized files; all the records are located in separate departments. But in well-managed businesses, even though records are decentralized, an executive is appointed to control and be responsible for filing systems and procedures for the entire organization. Such an arrangement is known as *decentralized records under centralized control,* and it has many of the advantages of both centralized and departmental files. For example, with this arrangement, filing can be done by full-time workers who go from one department to another, as they are needed. At the same time, records are economically located nearest the point of actual use.

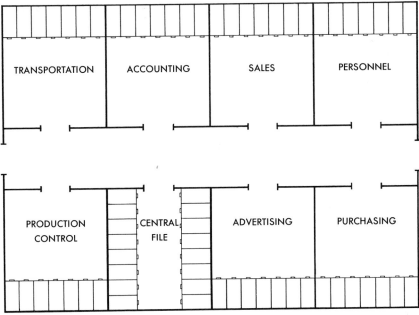

Floorplan of a Company Having Both Centralized and Departmental Files

1. When records need to be well protected and controlled.

2. When records are used by more than one department and need to be easily located—not rounded up from several other departments.

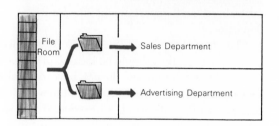

3. When duplication of records, space, equipment, or supplies needs to be eliminated in order to save money.

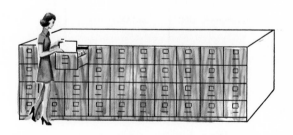

4. When filing can be done by full-time, professional file workers who can put filing on a production basis.

5. When all procedures can be standardized, making it easy to file, find, request, deliver, and return records to the files.

When Records Should Be Kept in Centralized Files

1. When records are confidential and should be available only to the department needing them.

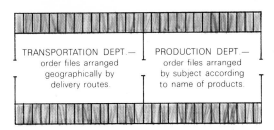

TRANSPORTATION DEPT.— order files arranged geographically by delivery routes.

PRODUCTION DEPT.— order files arranged by subject according to name of products.

2. When copies of the same records are filed differently according to how the using department calls for them.

Purchasing Department

Sales Department

3. When space for an adequate, well-staffed, and well-equipped centrally located file room is not available.

4. When fast, immediate reference to records is necessary.

5. When it is economical to locate records nearest the point of most frequent use.

When Records Should Be Kept in Departmental Files

In a small organization where there may be only one office or only a few offices not organized on a departmental basis, the following questions should be asked before deciding where to locate the files.   These questions also help to determine in which department records of a large organization should be kept.

1.   What Space Is Available?   File cabinets, for example, should not be placed so that a passageway is blocked when a drawer is pulled open.

2.   Who Uses Each Type of Record Most Frequently?   Customers' records, for example, should be near the accounts receivable clerk; credit records, near the credit manager.

3.   How Are Records Used?   Files of address plates should be near the addressing machine, the ledgers should be near the accounting machine, and the price list files near a telephone.

4.   How Does Each Type of Record Fit into the Work Flow?   As an example, if the billing clerk is the last person to handle an incoming order before it is filed, then the incoming order file should be near his desk.

When the questions have been answered, the file worker is ready to make the next important decision: how should the records be classified?

How Should the Records Be Classified?

Whether records should be classified alphabetically, numerically, geographically, by subject, or by date sometimes depends entirely on how the records are most frequently called for.   But because some records may be called for in a number of ways and because certain systems have advantages over others for a given job, all filing systems should be carefully considered.   A useful device in making the decision of which system to use is the Filing System Selection Chart on page 181.

Using the Filing System Selection Chart

1.   Prepare a Chart.   For each type of record that will have a separate location or filing system, prepare a chart similar to the sample.   Write the type of record in the block at the upper left.

2.   Answer the Questions.   Answer the 15 questions by placing a check in one of the two columns under *Answer.*

FILING SYSTEM SELECTION CHART

Type of record: *Job Applications* Department: *Personnel* Date: *May 17, 19--*

Question	Answer YES	Answer NO*	ALPHA-BETIC	NUMERIC	GEO-GRAPHIC	SUBJECT
			If answer is "Yes," use this system. If answer is "No," disregard.			
1. Is necessity for occasional reference to an index undesirable?		√	📁			
2. Should the filing system be direct?	√		📁		📁	📁
3. Should expansion be unlimited?	√			📁		📁
4. Should there be a provision for miscellaneous records?		√	📁	📁	📁	
5. Should the system provide for grouping of records of the same individual or company?		√	📁	📁	📁	
6. Should the system provide for grouping of records by location?		√			📁	
7. Should the system provide for grouping of records by topic?	√					📁
8. Is permanent and liberal cross-reference needed?		√		📁		
9. Is an index or list of all correspondents and subjects needed?	√			📁	📁	📁
10. Is filing accuracy of unusual importance?		√		📁		
11. Is minimum filing labor cost of unusual importance?		√	📁			
12. Is ease of coding of unusual importance?		√	📁	📁	📁	
13. Are positive identification numbers needed for records?		√		📁		
14. Is a minimum of cross-referencing desirable?	√		📁			
15. Is it particularly important to avoid congestion under common names such as Smith?		√		📁		
Totals *or unimportant			2	2	2	4

A large manufacturing firm used this chart in deciding to file job applications by subject.

3. Count "Yes" Answers. Starting from the top of the column headed *Alphabetic*, move your finger down the column, counting the number of small folders that are beside *Yes* answers. Do not count folders that are beside *No* answers. Place the total count in the square at the bottom of the column. Repeat this count for the other three columns.

4. Choose a System. Use the totals as a guide in choosing the filing system. Usually the filing system having the highest total will be the most satisfactory one to install, but sometimes a filing system that does not have the highest total will be the best one to use because of the extreme importance of one or two questions. Therefore, examine the other columns carefully to see whether some important *Yes* answers indicate that a system with a low total should be used.

Flexibility, Expansion, and Distribution

Regardless of which filing system is selected, it should provide for flexibility, expansion, and proper distribution of records. *Flexibility* in a filing system means that the filing system may be changed as the work load and work flow of an office change. Many filing systems that were once efficient become bogged down and actually slow the flow of office work. For example, in the office of a gas company, a bad-debts card file is maintained. This file lists names and amounts owed by customers who have moved away from the city without paying their gas bills. When a person or an organization applies for gas service, this file is searched to see whether the applicant owes money from previous service. The file apparently served its purpose for many years, before deposits were required of customers who did not own their own property. The office manager would be wise, however, to compare the cost of maintaining it with the income from payment of old bills (some of them 25 years past due). He might find that maintaining it for an indefinite period is a serious burden on the firm in terms of expense, time, and space.

Expansion in a filing system means making some provision for the increasing numbers of records that result from the growth of the organization. For example, as the number of credit customers of a business increases, more customer accounts must be kept. Expansion can be provided for by either using systems that are easily expanded, such as subject and numeric, or by providing space in whatever system is used, such as alphabetic, in anticipation of increased numbers of records. For example, an alphabetic file will allow for expansion if, when it is first set up, file drawers are not filled to capacity. If there are empty drawers, they should not be at the end of the alphabet but should be interspersed to allow for expansion, as illustrated on page 183. Some files can be expanded easily if the cabinets are of the same make

How Proper Placement of Empty File Drawers in a New System Permits Expansion

Poor	Better

Poor

A–C	M–O		
D–F	P–R		
G–I	S–T		
J–L	U–Z		

Expanding these files requires that most of the records be moved.

Better

A–C	G–I	M–O	S–T
D–F	J–L	P–R	U–Z

These files provide for easy expansion.

and have drawers that are removable. Rather than move records from one drawer to another, a worker can move the whole drawer from one cabinet to another. However, if a file drawer is full of heavy records, a worker should not attempt to remove it by himself.

Proper distribution of records means that the most frequently referred-to records are evenly distributed throughout the files and that the relative number of records is about the same in each filing location. Without proper distribution of records, file workers get in one another's way when storing and finding records and certain sections of the files become overcrowded while other sections contain unused space. Probably one of the best solutions to poor records distribution would result from the installation of a terminal-digit filing system.

What Should Be the Arrangement of Files?

The proper setup of a good records management system depends upon the arrangement, or layout, of files for a smooth flow of work and a thrifty use of space. Efficient layout takes into account (1) the sequence of work in the file area, (2) the space required for files, (3) the frequency of reference, and (4) the problems of supervision. Other, more technical, problems of layout are discussed in office management books and will not be taken up in this text. Because standard correspondence file cabinets outnumber other types, they will be used here to illustrate the principles of efficient file layout.

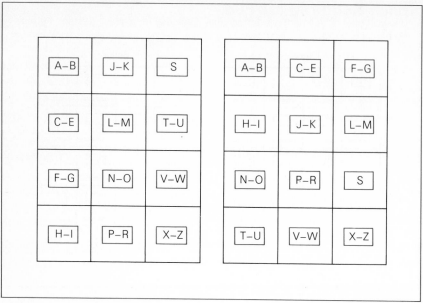

Vertical labeling of file drawers, left, is most common.   Horizontal labeling, right, is preferred for some operations.

Adjustment to Work Flow

As you learned in Chapter 1, every office has a definite work routine. Since the purpose of files is to help control and organize office work, they must first be arranged to fit work patterns. A conscientious file worker, then, will ask first the question, "How can the files be arranged to best serve the *whole office?*" Only then will he be concerned with the question, "How can the files be arranged to make *my* work easiest?" This is an important principle in file layout: *The files should fit the flow of office work, not vice versa.*

To fit the work flow in most offices, the order of the contents of files is from top to bottom in the cabinet. This is known as vertical labeling of drawers. File drawers may also be labeled horizontally, as illustrated above. From cabinet to cabinet the order is usually left to right. Probably the easiest way to arrange a series of related file cabinets is to back them up in a straight line along a wall. But for large file systems or small rooms, the straight line is not always possible or practical. For example, straight-line files might require too much walking. Other schemes that might better fit space and work flow are rows of files lined up back to back, with aisles between facing drawers; a cluster, or island, of files in the center of a room; a rectangle of files that encloses a work area; and a row of files extending perpendicularly to a wall. Four arrangements are illustrated on page 188.

Space Required for Files

A major cost of filing is the price a businessman has to pay for floor space for filing equipment. Intelligent arrangement of file cabinets will keep the space used—and the cost—to a minimum. A wise step in file arrangement is to figure the floor area needed for the files. The area needed for one cabinet when the drawer is completely open is about six square feet. Thus, the total square footage of floor space needed for the files can be figured easily—six times the number of file cabinets. (Six square feet is only an approximate figure, because file cabinets vary in depth by as much as five inches.) Next, the arrangement of the files is determined. Many file workers make a simple scale drawing of the filing area and then place cutouts, called *templates*, of scale-size filing cabinets on the drawing to help them visualize the best arrangement. It is, of course, much easier to rearrange templates than heavy file cabinets. These templates are provided free by some filing supply companies; they can also be easily made. Doll-house-type models or scale drawings of file cabinets are sometimes used instead of templates.

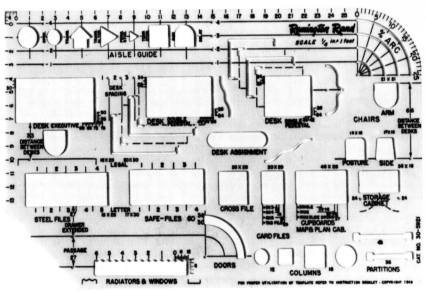

Courtesy Remington Rand

A template is used to draw office furniture in planning an office layout.

Frequency of Reference

Frequency of reference must be considered before a decision is made on the width of aisles between cabinets. To save space in storage areas where inactive papers are filed, the aisles may be as narrow as 30 inches, or the

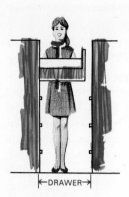

Minimum for Storage Area

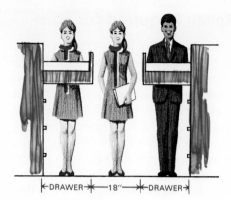

Minimum for Active Files

Preferred for Storage Area

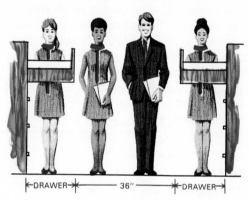

Preferred for Active Files

Minimum and Preferred Aisle Widths

depth of one drawer. A better arrangement, if space is available, is to also include space for passage (18 inches) when a file drawer is opened into the aisle. For active files, aisles should be at least wide enough to permit facing drawers to be fully extended and to provide an additional 18 inches for passage. Preferred for active files, however, is a passageway for two file workers (36 inches) when facing drawers are extended. The use of open-shelf files decreases the amount of aisle space needed because it is not necessary to make allowance for the opening of file drawers into the aisles.

Supervisory Problems

The layout of files is extremely important to a file supervisor. He must be stationed near enough to the files to be certain that charge procedures are followed, and the files should be arranged so that the aisles are open, insofar

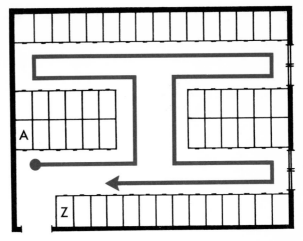

These files are arranged for a minimum of walking.

as possible, to his view. Conversely, cabinets should be partitioned off from office workers who are not authorized to use them. (Sometimes the files themselves are arranged to form partitions.)

Long rows of cabinets should have gaps to permit workers to save time by making shortcuts from one row to another. This also makes it convenient for the supervisor to make frequent spot checks on the file drawers and charge-out forms, and it permits him to assist file workers readily.

Organizing Records for Business Systems

The four basic questions enumerated at the beginning of this chapter have each been discussed. However, the final answers to such questions are difficult to formulate in an actual business situation without considering the overall purpose of the administrative operation for which the records are kept. Let us now see how these questions might be handled within the framework of two sample business systems: a personnel operation in a large manufacturing firm and a property rental and sales operation in a medium-size real estate company. These examples have been adapted from actual records management practices in the types of operations named.

Organizing Records in a Personnel Operation

The Daniel Manufacturing Corporation produces parts for electric motors and generators. About 2,000 employees work for this company, located in a city of 150,000 people. The personnel manager, R. M. Wisman, is responsible for managing all records relating to the 2,000 workers and for administering the employee suggestion program and employee welfare activities. Although other records are processed and stored in the personnel department, the

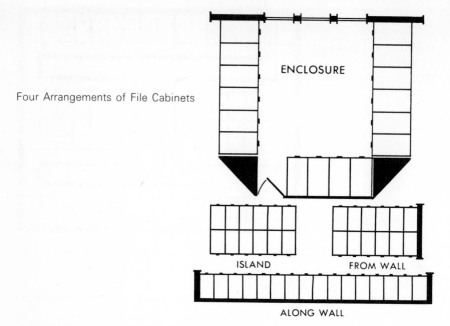

Four Arrangements of File Cabinets

ENCLOSURE

ISLAND   FROM WALL

ALONG WALL

following seven types of records constitute the great majority of the paper work handled by that department.

1. Prospective employee applications
2. Reference index of employees
3. Employee histories
4. Job descriptions
5. Employee medical records
6. Records of employee suggestions
7. General correspondence

Each of the seven classifications of records uses a separate filing system of some type. However, the decisions to be made concerning the organization and location of each type of record can be made only when the relationship of one record to another is understood. The chart on page 189 shows in simplified form how each type of record is related to the overall system of work in the personnel department.

Refer to the flowchart as you read the following descriptions of the seven types of records listed above. Each of the seven types is identified in the flowchart.

1. *Prospective employee applications.* These are stored in a subject-numeric file under 23 numbered job categories. When a hiring department needs a new employee in one of these categories, the personnel department workers can quickly determine whether a matching application is on file. Should an applicant be called for by name, an alphabetic card index to this

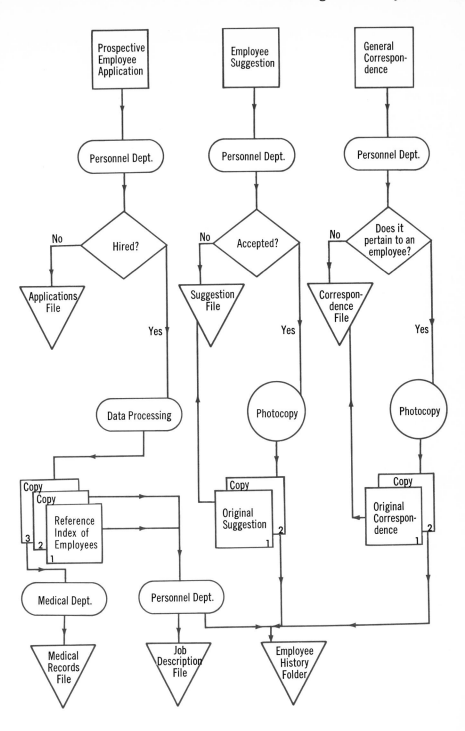

file is kept near the file. The records are stored near the desk of the clerk who administers tests and checks applications for completeness.

2. *Reference index of employees.* This list is kept on bound sheets printed on data processing equipment. The index has four parts in which all employees are listed (1) alphabetically by name, (2) alphabetically by job title, (3) numerically by payroll number, and (4) chronologically by date of employment. The index is kept near the desk of the personnel manager.

3. *Employee histories.* The employee history folders contain the employee's original job application, an employee data sheet, test results, ratings by supervisor, history of employment, progress reports, disciplinary action reports, salary records, birth certificate affidavit, and approved employee suggestions. A Variadex alphabetic file contains one history folder for each employee. There are no miscellaneous folders. The files are centrally located in the personnel department to permit easy access by most department workers.

4. *Employee job descriptions* are kept in two *tub* files. Because workers are rehired or temporarily released first on the basis of job category and then according to seniority, the first of these files is arranged numerically by job classification. Within each job classification, cards are arranged chronologically according to date of original employment. The second tub file contains duplicates of the 2,000 cards in the first file, but the cards are arranged alphabetically by employee name. This file is referred to when the personnel workers are looking for job information concerning a specific employee. Both files are located centrally in the personnel department so that they may be easily accessible for most department workers.

5. *Employee medical records,* although considered to be personnel records, are filed in the infirmary, where they are most often needed. It is not a coincidence, however, that the infirmary is located next to the personnel department in the administrative wing of the plant. The records are organized alphabetically by employee name, each worker having an individual folder.

6. *Records of employee suggestions.* A separate folder is kept in the employee suggestions file for each department in the plant. It is a subject file arranged by department name, and within each folder suggestions are arranged chronologically. A copy of each accepted suggestion is also filed in the employee's history folder. Management uses this file for overall and departmental evaluation of the employee suggestion program. The file is kept conveniently close to the personnel manager's secretary, who maintains it.

7. *General correspondence.* Incoming general correspondence and copies of outgoing correspondence are filed alphabetically in folders in a standard vertical correspondence file. The secretary to the personnel manager is responsible for the maintenance of this file, so the file is located near her desk. Correspondence related to a particular employee is photocopied; the copy is stored in the employee's history folder, and the original is filed in the general correspondence file.

Organizing Records for a Property Rental and Sales Operation

Harris Realty Company, located in a city of 500,000 people, performs the following primary services: (1) it sells property listed with it by clients; (2) it rents and leases property listed with it by clients. The profits earned by Harris Realty come from commissions received from the sale and rental of real estate. The following nine kinds of records are most important for the management of the rental and sales operations of the firm.

1. Listings of property for sale
2. Listings of property for rent
3. Requests for property to be purchased
4. Requests for property to be rented
5. Maps
6. Keys
7. Contracts
8. Closing statements
9. Accounting records

Just as with the previous example, each of the nine classifications of records has a separate filing system at Harris Realty.

1. *Listings of property for sale.* Each listing includes type of property (house, apartment, store, lot), location, name and address of owner, price, description, and age of property. Data is kept on 5- by 3-inch cards in a subject-geographic card file. Primary guides are for type of property (business, residental, industrial, etc.), and secondary guides are for area and address within each primary classification. The file is referred to as a master sales-listing file, and it is kept on the office manager's desk during the day and in a fireproof safe at night. Each salesman has a duplicate of this file in his own loose-leaf notebook.

2. *Listings of property for rent.* Although these listings are kept in a file separate from sales listings, they are organized in the same manner as the sales listings.

3. *Requests for property to be purchased.* These records include the name of the potential buyer, the type of property wanted, the desired location, and the approximate price he is willing to pay. Two 5- by 3-inch card files are kept: (1) A subject-geographic file with primary guides for the type of property and with secondary guides for the area. (2) A card file with cross-references to the above file, arranged alphabetically by the name of the person requesting the property. Files are referred to as prospect files, and these files are kept on the office manager's desk. Individual salesmen keep duplicate cards only for prospects for which they are responsible.

4. *Requests for property to be rented.* Although these listings are kept in a file separate from purchase requests, they are organized in the same manner as the purchase requests.

AREA OF CITY	STREET	NUMBER	PRICE
S.W.	Jefferson	17	$45,000
OWNER-LAST NAME FIRST MIDDLE			PHONE NO.
Jones, Henry D.			237-6812
STREET ADDRESS OR R.F.D. NO.		CITY STATE	
18 Main St.		Peekskill N.Y.	
TENANT-LAST NAME FIRST MIDDLE			PHONE NO.
POSSESSION DATE	TERMS	TAXES	SEE REVERSE FOR PROPERTY → DESCRIPTION
Immediate	25% cash	$1100	

A real estate firm records houses and other property for sale on this 5- by 3-inch card, which is filed under type of property.

TYPE OF PROPERTY WANTED	PRICE RANGE
Motel site	$40,000-$50,000
AREA OF CITY	POSSESSION DATE
Springwood Park	Summer
NAME-LAST FIRST MIDDLE	PHONE NO.
Fitzgerald, James W.	418-2175
STREET ADDRESS OR R.F.D. NO.	CITY STATE
80 Willow Court	Hamilton Vt.
DESCRIPTION OF PROPERTY WANTED (SIZE, SPECIAL FEATURES) Approx. 10 acres near interstate	
interchange. Will buy or lease.	

Filed by subject, this 5- by 3-inch prospect card keeps needs of prospective real estate buyers at salesmen's fingertips.

5. *Maps* of streets and lots covering the entire area the company serves are kept on file. They are arranged geographically by name of subdivision. A card index to the maps is organized by street names, names of owners, and city tax numbers. The maps themselves are kept in large loose-leaf *map books,*

which are easily accessible to the salesmen. The books are stored horizontally in drawers.

6. *Keys* to homes, buildings, and apartments that are for rent or for sale are kept so that property can be shown to prospects. Keys are organized on a vertical *key board* geographically by street name and number. Keys are *charged out* by salesmen, and are kept near a door leading to a parking lot behind the office building.

7. *Contracts* and correspondence regarding sales, rentals, or leases for which a contract has been written are filed alphabetically by the name of the seller and cross-referenced under the name of the buyer. They are kept in a contract file, which is permanently located in a large fireproof vault near the accountant's office.

8. *Closing statements.* Both purchaser's and seller's closing statements, which summarize amounts of money to be paid and by whom, are organized alphabetically in a correspondence file by name of purchaser and seller. This file is located between the office manager and the accountant.

9. *Accounting records.* Customer accounts and accounts with creditors are arranged in two separate sections of a visible loose-leaf binder. These records are stored at the accountant's work station during working hours. At other times they are stored in the vault.

Questions and Problems

1. What basic decisions must be made when planning a records system?
2. What factors are considered in determining whether a record should be filed?
3. What are centralized files? departmental files?
4. What are decentralized records under centralized control?
5. What factors are considered in determining where a record should be filed?
6. Prepare a Filing System Selection Chart similar to the one on page 181 for each of the following:
   a. Purchase invoices
   b. Job application letters
   c. Salesmen's reports about calls on customers
7. What is meant by *flexibility and expansion* in a filing system?
8. What should be the first consideration in file layout?
9. Describe horizontal and vertical labeling of file drawers.
10. What are several ways to arrange file cabinets in an office?
11. What are templates used for?
12. In what way does frequency of reference affect the width of aisles between files?
13. How should files be arranged to provide for good supervision?

14. Describe the records system of a typical personnel department.
15. Describe the records system of a typical real estate office.

Case Problems in Records Management

1. The Blake E. Hadley Corporation, an organization with over 1,000 employees on its payroll, has a records system that is not meeting the company's needs. Should an outside consultant be hired to modernize its system; or should the filing department supervisor, a competent individual who has had seven years' experience with the company, be given the assignment?

2. Organize a system for filing the academic records of your graduating class. Be specific in your recommendations for primary and secondary captions.

3. Organize a system for filing the records of an instructor who teaches several business subjects.

4. Organize a system for filing recipes and other kitchen records.

5. Karen Fuller, file supervisor of Lovely Lady Cosmetics, Inc., is considering moving the invoice files downstairs from the second-floor accounting department to the central files so that control of these records will be easier for her. What other factors should Miss Fuller consider?

6. Several records have been lost from the files of the Bell-Kirk Company in the past several weeks. The files are arranged in rows in the center of a large room. The file supervisor has noticed recently that office workers from the accounting department take shortcuts between the rows of files as they go to and from their desks. What could be the cause of some of the file losses? What might prevent such losses?

Evaluating Records Systems and Personnel

BECAUSE RECORDS ARE SO VITAL to the operation and control of an enterprise, the success of a business may depend on the efficiency of records management. Frequent checkups on filing systems, procedures, office forms, and methods used by employees help to ensure maximum performance, minimum expense, and minimum time consumed. Can records be obtained promptly and economically? Or is filing and finding slow and expensive? Are office forms designed to provide information readily and accurately? Or are the forms awkward to fill in and difficult to obtain information from? These questions must be considered periodically.

Evaluation of the Filing Operation

Large firms that are cost-conscious and interested in filing efficiency make formal file evaluations regularly. Such businesses keep a record of the filing activity in the organization through daily, weekly, or monthly volume reports. These reports show the total number of records filed, the number of records requested from the files, and the number that were found and not found. This information is sometimes listed separately for each file worker for individual evaluation, then totaled to evaluate the performance of the entire force. The evaluation is made either by comparing present performance with past performance or by determining the *activity ratio* or the *accuracy ratio.*

195

Activity Ratio

The activity ratio, or percent of filed records requested, lets the file worker or supervisor know whether too many records are being kept in the active files. The formula for the ratio is:

$$\frac{\text{Requests for records}}{\text{Number of records in active files}} = \text{Activity ratio}$$

If 20,000 records are in the files and 5,000 are requested from them during a filing period, the activity ratio for that period is:

$$\frac{5,000}{20,000} = 25\% \text{ activity ratio}$$

If the activity ratio is higher than 20 percent, it is more than likely that the files do not contain too many unnecessary records. If the ratio is between 10 and 20 percent, some of the records in the active files probably should be transferred. An activity ratio below 10 percent means that many records in the active files should be transferred to storage.

Accuracy Ratio

The accuracy ratio, or percent of requested records found, is a good indication of the efficiency of both the filing system and employee work routines. The formula is as follows:

$$\frac{\text{Records found}}{\text{Records requested}} = \text{Accuracy ratio}$$

If 3,000 records are requested and 2,940 are found during a filing period, the accuracy ratio for that period is:

$$\frac{2,940}{3,000} = 98\% \text{ accuracy ratio}$$

If the accuracy ratio is higher than 99.5 percent, filing can be considered very efficient. A ratio under 97 percent is an indication that attention should be given to one or more of the following: indexing and coding, cross-referencing, storing procedures, charge-out and follow-up, routine procedures to and from the files, and checking on unnecessary retention of records in employees' desks.

Evaluation of File-Worker Performance

Large organizations also evaluate the performance of their file employees. Because file work varies a great deal from company to company, evaluations are usually based on the firm's own experience—not on general standards. The following examples of performance standards established by Record Controls, Inc., are based on surveys of several hundred firms:

FILING PROCEDURES	PIECES PER HOUR
Sorting and filing cards alphabetically	200
Filing cards alphabetically (previously sorted to exact sequence)	320
Reading, coding, and rough sorting correspondence for alphabetic file	300
Rough sorting papers in flat sorter	750
Filing correspondence (previously sorted) in alphabetic file	250
Finding and removing papers from correspondence file	80
Sorting papers in exact sequence for a numeric file	700
Filing papers numerically (previously sorted)	450
Sorting papers in exact sequence for a terminal-digit numeric file	280
Filing papers numerically in a terminal-digit arrangement (previously sorted)	380
Filing papers in a geographic file	200
Classifying and filing records by subject	100
Typing and affixing folder labels	30

Evaluation of File Equipment

Evaluation of filing efficiency must also include a systematic study of file equipment and supplies. In many firms such a study has led to the installation of open-shelf files, a very popular development in recent years. An open-shelf file is illustrated on page 198. Note that there are no drawers in the file. Because the space necessary for pulling out file drawers is eliminated and because the file may be eight or nine shelves in height, open-shelf files save up to 50 percent of the floor space needed for ordinary files. They are much less expensive, too, not only in the original cost but in the time required for filing and finding records. Open-shelf files are recommended for very large active files when there is space enough to house them away from public view. They are also very effective for inactive records that have been transferred from the active files. Switching to open-shelf files can often relieve crowded conditions in the files of a large company.

A thorough evaluation of filing supplies will reveal whether the proper number of filing guides is contained in each drawer—usually between 20 and 40. This number will usually provide proper distribution of records, make reference to the files easy, and furnish support for the folders.

Remington Rand suggests the following proportion of guides to drawer space and correspondence:

DRAWERS OF CORRESPONDENCE	NUMBER OF PAPERS FILED	NUMBER OF GUIDES REQUIRED
1	up to 4,000	20–40
2	4,000–6,000	40–60
3	6,000–8,000	60–80
4	8,000–10,000	80–100
5–6	10,000–15,000	100–150
7–8	15,000–20,000	150–200
9–12	20,000–30,000	200–300
13–16	30,000–40,000	300–400
17–20	40,000–50,000	400–500
21–24	50,000–60,000	500–600
25–28	60,000–80,000	600–800
29–36	80,000–100,000	800–1,000

In many organizations, automation has had an effect on equipment, supplies, and procedures. Cards and magnetic tape are used for recording information. Instead of printed words and figures, information takes the form of punched holes or magnetic impulses. These tapes and cards must be stored for later use, and they require special storage equipment. Some of the equipment used for these types of records is illustrated on pages 132 and 134 in Chapter 9.

Courtesy Tab Products Company

A Well-Organized Open-Shelf File

Small Organization Checkups

Compared with large firms, small organizations make less formal and less detailed filing evaluations. Their studies usually include a committee discussion of filing procedures and suggestions for improvements and close attention to a checklist by the person responsible for records management. Such a checklist questions every phase of filing operations:

1. Is the filing system proper for the function the records have?
2. Are the records given the required protection against fire, theft, and dampness?
3. Are records filed daily or more often if necessary?
4. Are important records being "filed" in desk drawers or trays?
5. Are useless materials being filed?
6. Are there many instances of misfiled or lost records?
7. Are there new developments in equipment or supplies that will improve operations?
8. Are file drawers overcrowded?
9. Is there an adequate number of guides (at least 20) for each drawer?
10. Is an individual folder prepared when five or more papers accumulate from one correspondent?
11. Is the number of papers in any standard folder limited to a maximum of 100?
12. When papers need fastening within a folder, are staples rather than pins or paper clips used?
13. Do the file drawers, guides, and folders bear descriptive labels and captions?
14. Are standard indexing rules used?
15. Is there adequate cross-referencing?
16. Are the records properly coded?
17. Are the records sorted in the best way before storing?
18. Is there a charge-out and follow-up system that is used properly by all employees?
19. Is there adequate provision for transfer and disposal?
20. Is there a manual that describes the filing operations of the business?

If these twenty checklist questions are answered and the shortcomings they reveal corrected once each filing period (just before transfer time), files are likely to remain in efficient working condition. Even in the one-employee office, frequent attention to such a list can mean the difference between a neat, businesslike atmosphere and a desk full of disorganized papers.

For any size business in which filing efficiency is very low or in which records management is a problem, it is advisable to use the knowledge and experience of outside consulting organizations. One such firm has clients that range from multimillion-dollar corporations to one-man, one-room business operations. This firm not only gives advice on how to store records and dispose of them but also sells filing equipment and supplies.

Forms Analysis

As you learned in Chapter 4, forms are important carriers of business information and are the kind of record most often used in offices. Forms analysis is the process of deciding whether a business form is needed and, if so, what static information it should contain in what sequence and design. Both the selection of new forms and the improvement of old ones require forms analysis. An intelligent forms analysis includes, besides evaluation of individual forms, consideration of the relationship of one form to another in the entire flow of work in the organization. Factors that will be considered in the following discussion of forms analysis are: (1) investigating the need for the form, (2) providing for maximum readability, (3) providing for efficient filling out of the form, (4) providing for transmittal of the form, and (5) planning for the storage of the form.

Investigating the Need

A form is likely to be needed whenever repetitive information is required, such as *number of days absent* on an employee leave request. Also, when standard facts are required, such as the birth date of employees, and when these facts must be organized for fast processing, forms are extremely useful. But good records managers know that forms should not be created unless there is a definite need, because the cost of processing forms is estimated to be fifteen to twenty times the cost of printing them. A business form is not necessary and can be eliminated if (1) the information it supplies is not used, (2) another source of information is available, or (3) the cost of the form (largely the labor cost of filling it in) exceeds its value. Very often forms ask for needless information. For example, a form might ask for a person's age and date of birth, when only one of these would do. Therefore, when forms are being designed or evaluated, the question, "How will this information be used?" should be asked for each item.

When more than one copy of a form is needed, *multiple copies* are made by means of carbons or chemically treated paper. Even though multiple copies save the labor costs of additional writing, a wise forms analyst will question the need for them. There are at least three pitfalls in preparing too many extra copies: (1) waste of paper; (2) loss of employee time in handling, reading, and filing copies; and (3) waste of valuable filing space.

Investigating the need for forms or parts of them does not always mean eliminating or combining forms, items, or copies, but sometimes a form can be improved by a split-up into two or more new ones. In other cases, additional forms, items, or copies might improve work flow in the office.

Providing for Maximum Readability

Readability is important because the purpose of a form is to provide accurate, readily accessible information that can be used to make correct business decisions. The person filling in the form must understand it before he can give the desired information. Techniques that improve readability of a form include the following:

1. *Titles* should be short and should indicate the purpose of a form. The words *form, sheet,* or *record* in a title are usually unnecessary. Compare these titles:
   a. Inventory Card Record for Files
   b. Factory Supplies Inventory
2. *Captions* (or questions) should be adapted to the background of the user of the form, and they should make responses easy—leaving no doubt as to what information is wanted. Compare these:

Example A
  What is your name and address?
  What is your age?
  How tall are you?
  How much do you weigh?
  What color are your eyes?

Example B

PRINT FULL NAME	FIRST	MIDDLE	LAST

PRINT STREET ADDRESS OR R. F. D. NO.

PRINT CITY AND STATE

MONTH BORN	YEAR BORN	HEIGHT FT. IN.	WEIGHT	COLOR OF EYES

In Example B each item is blocked off for ease of reading and correct placement of data. Before a form is printed, readability should first be tested by having potential users fill in sample copies.

3. Most forms require accompanying *instructions*. When they are brief, such as "Print full name" in the example on page 201, they may be on the form itself. When they are lengthy or complex, instructions should be printed on the back of the form or in a separate manual that includes a filled-in sample illustration of the form.

Providing for Efficient Writing

Well-designed forms are easy to fill in, whether information is entered by hand or machine. Such forms reduce possibilities of error in recording the data, and they speed the writing process. Factors to be considered in "writability" are sequencing, spacing, and construction.

Sequencing

The sequence of items on a form should be determined by traditional reading habits, relation of the form to other forms, and frequency of use. People are accustomed to reading left to right, top to bottom. They are also used to seeing related items in a standard order, such as an address given first by house number, then by street, city, state, and ZIP Code. For fast processing of data, all items that are on related forms should be in the same sequence on all those forms. Items that are filled in on all the forms should be first; any that are not always filled in are placed at the right; those filled in on only a few of the forms should be at the bottom.

Boxes (commonly called *ballot boxes*) are used when a question may be answered *yes* or *no* or when a selection of answers can be listed. Contrast the following:

Example A

List the sports you are qualified to coach:

Example B

Check the sports you are qualified to coach:

☐ football   ☐ baseball   ☐ soccer   ☐ other_____

☐ basketball   ☐ track   ☐ tennis   ☐ other_____

Example B has the following advantages over Example A: Less space is used, less writing time is required, the user is reminded of possible answers, the answers are uniform in wording and position, and the chances of error are reduced.

Spacing

Forms filled in by hand should have writing spaces at least $\frac{1}{4}$ inch high for desk work and $\frac{1}{3}$ inch high for field work, such as surveying or delivering. Horizontal space should be adequate for the information to be written in neatly.

For the design or improvement of forms to be typewritten, these facts about most standard typewriters must be considered: There are 6 vertical spaces per inch, there are 12 horizontal spaces per inch on elite-type machines and 10 on pica-type machines, and it is usually more efficient if the tabulator rather than the space bar can be used for moving from one item to another.

There are three basic spacing designs for handwritten or typewritten forms:

1. Caption on or under the line of writing:

```
Ship via
```

```
Ship via
```

2. Box design:

```
Ship via
```

3. Column arrangement:

```
                    Ship via
```

Each has its particular advantages or disadvantages. When captions are on the line of writing, the typist filling in the form must space through the printed words to reach the next typing position. Captions under the line are satisfactory for forms filled in by hand, but below-the-line captions are hidden on a typewriter. The box design, with captions printed in small type in the upper portion of the box, saves space and eliminates excessive typewriter spacing or adjustment. It also ensures correct placement of data. Column design facilitates the use of the typewriter tabulator. This design is especially useful when many numbers, such as prices of goods, are to be entered.

Construction

The three basic kinds of forms construction are single sheets, pads (or tablets), and specialty forms. Regardless of the kind used, standard sizes should be used whenever possible so special equipment or supplies will not be needed for writing, mailing, and filing the form.

The single sheet is the most widely used type because it can be filled in by hand or by machine, and it can be printed economically on any kind of paper. Single sheets can be folded and perforated in a variety of ways.

Pads of forms have these advantages: (1) forms are kept in alignment for carbon insertion, especially when they are handwritten; (2) when blank forms are transported often, the pad prevents them from wrinkling and becoming dog-eared, which can easily happen to single sheets; and (3) pads make possible the preassembly of *sets* when a series of different colors of the same form is to be used.

Specialty forms can be designed for any specific situation—for multiple copies, for special fastenings, for use in unique machines. They are usually produced as sets of copies with *one-time* (to be used only once) carbon sheets between forms. Specialty forms cost more than single sheets or pads, but

This form combines several basic spacing designs.

when they are properly used, the labor savings can more than offset their high price. One use of specialty forms is *selective copying*. This process is possible when a multiple form has carbon sheets with uncoated areas so that some of the information recorded on the first sheet is not copied on other sheets. Specialty forms are also available in various sets in which carbon sheets can be removed rapidly; in *masters,* copies of which can be run off on office duplicators; and in strips for use in accounting machines and sales registers.

Design for Smooth Transmittal

Forms analysts and records workers are concerned with how well an office form can be routed and dispatched to and from other departments or businesses. Within an organization the routing information can be put on the form itself, thereby eliminating routing slips or transmittal memorandums. If the form has multiple copies, papers of different colors can be used to signal which copy is to be sent to or kept by which department.

Forms that are mailed to other organizations should be designed to speed the addressing, collating, folding, and inserting steps that the form must go through. For example, if window envelopes are to be used, the form should be designed so that the address can be seen through the window without unusual folding of the form. Since it is often necessary to encourage the return of forms, they can be designed with *self-mailers*—they can be printed on postcards or on sheets that can be folded and fastened and then used as envelopes.

Design for Efficient Filing

There is an obvious relationship between the design of a form and the speed and accuracy of filing and finding it. First, if a study reduces the number of forms, there is a corresponding decrease in the amount of filing equipment and space needed, as well as a decrease in the number of hours spent in filing and finding. Second, if a form is designed to make handling and reading easy, there is an accompanying increase in filing efficiency.

When items on forms are not arranged for efficient filing, a situation such as the following might occur. An application form used at one time by a very large organization had the filing data—the applicant's name—in the center of the form. The forms were stored in vertical files in scores of branch offices across the country. In order to find an individual's application, it was necessary first to guess its probable location in the file. Clerks had to remove each form completely from the file and read the name, and this process had to be continued until the right application was reached. It took nine minutes, on the average, to find an application and only five minutes to process it.

VISUAL AIDS CORPORATION

Salesman's Report of Exhibits

Booth No. _____ Dates_____

Stock Exhibited (List) _____

Number Registered _____ Number of Requests for Materials _____

Date _____ Signature of Salesman _____

City and State _____ Name of Sponsoring Organization _____

VISUAL AIDS CORPORATION

Salesman's Report of Exhibits at _____

City and State	Booth No.	Dates
Was Material Distributed? ☐ Yes ☐ No	**If "Yes," Check Items Below**	
Films _____ Records _____ Filmstrips _____ Tapes _____	Visi-Guides _____ Recorders _____ Screens _____ Projectors _____	
Number Registered	Number of Requests for Materials	
Date	Signature of Salesman	

These two forms call for the same information, but they are designed differently. Which form would be easier to fill in? Which would give management more data?

If the name had been on the upper edge of the form, the correct application form could have been located in a fraction of a minute.

As a general rule, filing data on forms should be at the top when forms are filed vertically, at the visible edge when forms are filed in visible equipment, and at the side opposite the point of fastening when forms are bound. In making decisions as to placement of filing data, the following must be considered: In what type of equipment will the form be stored—standard file cabinet, open shelves, visible files, or other? Will the form be filed in folders or not? Will the form be fastened to other forms or papers? If so, where and with what type of fastener?

Size of Forms

Forms requiring other than standard-size filing cabinets can prove to be inefficient because of the extra cost of the equipment. Even legal-size cabinets cost more and occupy more space than standard letter-size ones. A small form can become hidden and difficult to find when filed with larger records. Likewise, a large form can take extra space and slow down file searching when it is folded to standard letter-size dimensions. Therefore, a form should usually be designed to have the same dimensions as the other records with which it will be stored.

Standard paper-mill sizes should also be considered before deciding on the size of a particular form. This will ensure minimum waste and lowest cost per form. The printer should be consulted for this information.

Properties of Paper Forms

Some of the properties of paper are weight, grade, and grain. The amount and kind of handling the form will receive should be considered when selecting the type of paper. If forms are frequently removed from and reinserted in files, used for posting of additional data, or transported a great deal, they should be able to resist wear and tear.

When considering weight, the lightest paper that will give satisfactory results should be used. Of course, the heavier weights are more durable. Standard weights recommended for various records are as follows:

RECORD	*WEIGHT OF 500 SHEETS IN POUNDS 17" x 22" BOND*
Legal documents	28
Ledgers	24
Letterheads or forms (single copy)	20
1–4 copies of multiple forms	16
5–8 copies of multiple forms	13
9 or more copies of multiple forms	tissue weight

In some large businesses records are prepared in several copies so that different departments may have their own copies. Notice that the same record is stored in three different ways, according to how it will be requested.

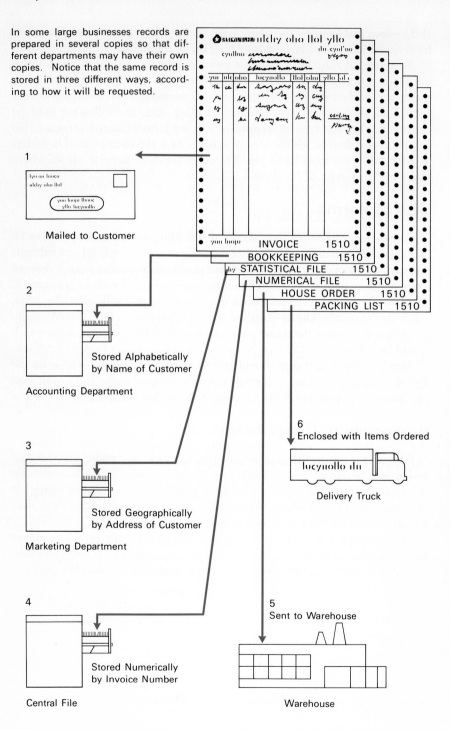

1

Mailed to Customer

2

Stored Alphabetically
by Name of Customer

Accounting Department

3

Stored Geographically
by Address of Customer

Marketing Department

4

Stored Numerically
by Invoice Number

Central File

5
Sent to Warehouse

Warehouse

6
Enclosed with Items Ordered

Delivery Truck

INVOICE   1510
BOOKKEEPING   1510
STATISTICAL FILE   1510
NUMERICAL FILE   1510
HOUSE ORDER   1510
PACKING LIST   1510

The grade of paper depends upon the ratio of fiber content to sulphite (wood pulp) content. The grade of paper recommended usually depends upon the life span of a form:

LIFE OF FORM	GRADE
1–5 Years	100% sulphite
6–12 Years	50% sulphite, 50% fiber
Over 12 Years	100% fiber

Most paper, like wood, has grain characteristics. The grain should run up and down on a form that is posted by machine and stored vertically so that the form will remain upright and not curl in a vertical tub or tray.

Questions and Problems

1. What questions must be considered in order to measure filing efficiency?
2. What information do volume reports contain?
3. Compare a large organization's evaluation with that of a small one.
4. Describe the activity ratio. How is it used?
5. Describe the accuracy ratio. How is it used?
6. What should be the primary basis for file-employee evaluation?
7. What are several advantages of open-shelf files?
8. Why is it important to have the proper number of file guides in a drawer?
9. How is information recorded on cards and tape for automated equipment?
10. What is an appropriate time to use a filing checklist?
11. What action should be taken if there is a serious records management problem?
12. What is meant by *forms analysis?*
13. Give three situations in which forms are not needed.
14. What are several results of preparing more copies of a form than are absolutely needed?
15. Does forms analysis necessarily mean the elimination or combination of forms, items on the form, or copies? Why?
16. What caution must be taken in the wording on forms?
17. How should lengthy or complex instructions for filling in forms be given?
18. What factors should determine the sequence of items on a form?
19. What advantages do ballot boxes have over blank lines on a form?
20. Describe the three basic spacing designs for forms.
21. What are the advantages of the box design over other spacing designs?
22. What type of form construction permits easy carbon insertion?
23. Describe several types of specialty forms.
24. Describe how selective copying is achieved.
25. How can color assist in the transmittal of forms?
26. What is a self-mailer?
27. How can forms design affect filing efficiency?

28. Where should filing data appear on vertically filed forms? on forms filed in visible equipment? on bound forms?
29. Name some factors to consider before deciding on the size of the form.
30. How are the properties of weight, grade, and grain decided upon for forms?

Case Problems in Records Management

1. The file supervisor of the Peerless Corporation is trying to convince the management that the policy of transferring the more capable members of his staff to other departments should be discontinued. He states that allowing him to increase the salaries within his department would enable him to get along with one less file worker and at the same time increase efficiency. He bases his claim on the following facts for the last filing period: number of records in active files—31,250; requests for records—2,500; records found—2,400. Compute the activity and accuracy ratios. Do they support his contention? Explain.

2. As an employee of the Visual Aids Corporation, you have been asked to redesign a report form for salesmen who exhibit at various meetings. Choose one of the two versions of this form on page 206, try to improve its design, and make a sketch of your own version. State the advantages in efficiency of your form over the old form.

3. Design a form that could be used for acquiring data to be printed next to each graduate's picture in the school yearbook. The questionnaire should remind each graduate of such items as activities in which he participated, postgraduation plans, and other pertinent information.

4. As an employee of the Carter Machine Corporation, you have been requested to help select the paper for a production department's foreman report form. The original copy of the form is to be retained for seven years, and two copies will be kept for one year each. The copies are to be sent to the shipping department and the accounting department, and the original is to be filed vertically in the foreman's office in the factory area. Make recommendations for the paper to be used for both the original and the copies of this form.

Appendix

Following are 17 exercises that apply the alphabetic indexing rules presented in Chapter 2. These exercises contain the same names as Jobs 1 through 17 in *Practice Materials for Filing Systems and Records Management, Second Edition.* Therefore, students who have practice materials need not complete the following exercises.

Exercise 1
After studying Alphabetic Indexing Rules 1–4:
A. Write each of the following names in correct indexing form on a separate 5- by 3-inch file card. The number before the name is to be placed in the upper right corner. For your guidance, the numbers of the appropriate alphabetic indexing rules have been placed beside each name.

1. Mary Da Mano[1,2,4]
2. Richard Barsto[1,2]
3. Herbert Avery[1,2]
4. A. Barker[1,2,3]
5. Evelyn L. Dittoe[1,2]

6. Albert Cooper[1,2]
7. George M. Ditto[1,2]
8. Henry U. Damano[1,2]
9. Barker[1,2,3]
10. Virgil De Berry[1,2,4]

Name *Young, Charles*	Exercise No. *1*
1. *3*	6.
2. *9*	7.
3. *4*	8.
4. *2*	9.
5.	10.

A Partially Completed Answer Sheet

211

B. Arrange the cards in correct alphabetic order.

C. On an answer sheet similar to the one illustrated on page 211, list the numbers on the file cards in the order in which they have been arranged. Hand in the answer sheet only.

D. Save the file cards for use in Exercise 14.

Exercise 2

After reviewing Alphabetic Indexing Rules 1–4:

Index and file cards for Names 11–20 and hand in an answer sheet. Save the file cards for use in Exercise 14.

11. George Du Bois[1,2,4]
12. Homer Anderson[1,2]
13. Carsons[1,2,3]
14. Edward Debee[1,2]
15. Geoffrey M. Du Bois[1,2,4]

16. Robert Barnhardt[1,2]
17. Vivian J. Churchill[1,2]
18. Josephine Carsons[1,2]
19. G. DuBois[1,2,3,4]
20. Joseph Carsons[1,2]

Exercise 3

After studying Alphabetic Indexing Rules 5–8:

Index and file cards for Names 21–30 and hand in an answer sheet. Save the file cards for use in Exercise 14.

21. Cooper-Walker Retreat Camp[5,8]
22. Jerry Burns Cab Company[6]
23. Albers Plumbing Company[5]
24. James Carlile-Simpson Importers[6,8]

25. Andy the Barber[5,7]
26. The Burns Agency[5,7]
27. Davenport Traders Market[5]
28. Adolph Cooper-Walker[8]
29. Carlile-Simpson Potteries[5,8]
30. The Sarah L. Albers Stylists[6,7]

Exercise 4

After reviewing Alphabetic Indexing Rules 1–8:

Index and file cards for Names 31–40 and hand in an answer sheet. Save the file cards for use in Exercise 14.

31. The Laura Adamson Salon[6,7]
32. Theodore Carter Garages[6]
33. The De Vleming Cooperative[4,5,7]
34. Barkley Development Company[5]

35. Buford-Field Library[8]
36. Isadore Barkley
37. De Lury Hatchery[4,5]
38. Barkley[3]
39. Harriet Buford-Field[8]
40. Rudolph Banning

Exercise 5

After studying Alphabetic Indexing Rules 9–12:

Index and file cards for Names 41–50 and hand in an answer sheet. Save the file cards for use in Exercise 14.

41. Cramer Lake Realty
    Brokers[12]
42. Fargo and Govertsen[10]
43. Adamson Mfg. Co.[9, 10]
44. Fargo and Govertsen Corp.[10]
45. Fargo-for-Gov. Club[8, 9, 10]

46. Fair Way Nursing Home[11]
47. Mary Adamson, Inc.[9, 10]
48. Cramer and Sons
    Contractors[10]
49. Fairway Golf Course[11]
50. Cramer of Detroit[10]

Exercise 6

After reviewing Alphabetic Indexing Rules 1–12:
Index and file cards for Names 51–60 and hand in an answer sheet.   Save
the file cards for use in Exercise 16.

51. De Coursey Radio Merchants[4]
52. Cowan Funeral Parlors Corp.[9, 10]
53. R. T. Decoursey
54. Desert & Western Airlines[10]
55. Buffalo Opera Co.[9, 10]
56. Buffalo-Eastern Bus Terminal[8]

57. Des Moines Evening News[12]
58. The Cowan-Fulton
    Clothing Co.[7, 8, 9, 10]
59. H. T. Cowan Company[6]
60. The Decoursey R.R.
    Supply Corp.[7, 10]

Exercise 7

After studying Alphabetic Indexing Rules 13–16:
Index and file cards for Names 61–70 and hand in an answer sheet.   Save
the file cards for use in Exercise 16.

61. Commander Estes[13]
62. Denmark Dept. of Educ.,
    Div. of Occupations[15]
63. City of De Lake Water
    Dept.[12, 16]
64. Commission for Development,
    Inc.[15]

65. Marion Este's Book Co.[6, 9, 10, 14]
66. Florence Dugan
67. Commerce Dept.,
    Washington, D.C.[15]
68. Henry Dugan, Jr.[13]
69. Estes' Machine Co.[14]
70. Dr. Henry Dugan[13]

Exercise 8

After reviewing Alphabetic Indexing Rules 1–16:
Index and file cards for Names 71–90 and hand in an answer sheet.   Save the
file cards for use in Exercise 16.

71. Acme Window Decorators,
    Ltd.[10]
72. Flynn's Art Gallery[14]
73. Eastside Bakeries[11]
74. De Leo's Boys Camp[4, 14]
75. Committee for the Blind[10, 15]
76. The Becker-Manning Club[7, 8]
77. ACM Motels[9]
78. Arthur N. Flynn and Sons[6, 10]
79. Dr. John R. Fiess, Chancellor[13]
80. Wm. W. Acme, Clothiers[6, 9]
81. Fiess' Cooperative[14]

82. D'Abbes'[3, 4, 14]
83. Homer A. Becker-Manning[8]
84. East Side Machine Mfrs.[9, 11]
85. F & R Escort Service[9, 10]
86. U.S. Dept. of Health,
    Educ., & Welfare[15]
87. The Henri R. D'Abbe
    Mart[4, 6, 7]
88. Carl's Car Wash[14]
89. Father Flynn[13]
90. State of Delaware, Bureau of
    Parks[16]

Exercise 9

After studying Alphabetic Indexing Rules 17–20:
Index and file cards for Names 91–100 and hand in an answer sheet. Save the file cards for use in Exercise 16.

91. The 4 Sailors' Oyster Bar[17]
92. Avery Industrials,
    9310 Fourth Street,
    Omaha, Nebraska 68120[18]
93. First Nat. Bank,
    Deerdorf, Idaho 83704[19]
94. Community Bank,
    Deerdorf, Idaho 83704[19]
95. Avery Industrials,
    Corvallis, Oregon 97330[18]

96. 4th Avenue Cleaners[17]
97. Crawford's Record Store[14]
98. Mrs. Theo. Crawford
    (Doris L.)[20]
99. Avery Industrials,
    1300 Fourth Street,
    Omaha, Nebraska 68117[18]
100. Mrs. Harold Crawford
    (Jane Smith)[20]

Complete Exercises 10–17 after (1) reviewing all alphabetic indexing rules and (2) studying the section on cross-referencing, pages 23–25.

Exercise 10

A. Place the following names (101–150) on cards in proper indexing order; then arrange them in the correct alphabetic sequence.

101. Richard Barbour, Sr.
102. Dorothy Bauer Shoppe
103. CGD Corporation
104. Christlieb Bakeries
105. B. Jerry Boorkman
106. The Ernest Burkley Fund
107. Erickson's Market,
    3246 Everett Street,
    Portland, Maine 00406
108. Eastside Budget Shop
109. Richard Barbour, Jr.
110. Helen Caplan Salon
111. State of Florida, Dept. of
    Labor
112. Behnke-Walker Business
    College
113. Doctor Culbertson
114. Eckhout-Wilmont Carting Co.
115. Thos. Fischer
116. Brenner's Shrubs
117. Chas. F. Berg's Store
118. Carsiding 17 Snack Bar
119. Du Pont Welders, Inc.
120. Citizens Bank of Du Pont
    Village, Florida
121. Ralph Bass
122. Captain Earl's Dock

123. The Boorkman Bros. Hatchery
124. Charles O. Behnke-Walker
125. Republic of France,
    Dept. of Labor
126. The Ralph Bass Agency
127. The D'Ascoli Infirmary
128. Eastern Savings Bank,
    Bandon, Alabama 35542
129. Erickson's Market,
    225 Everett Street,
    Portland, Maine 00404
130. Eckhout-Wilmont Corp.
131. Fisher the Plumber
132. Captain John H. Farmer
133. Elmira, Illinois, Chamber of
    Commerce
134. East-West Bus Co., Inc.
135. State of Arkansas,
    Bureau of Mines
136. Robert A. Farrand
137. Berg of Charleston
138. Alice F. Frank
139. Brazil Exporters
140. Fredrickson Kindergarten
141. Dorothy Du Baird
142. Genevieve Culbertson
143. Mrs. John Currier (Sarah K.)

144. Bergs
145. The 88 Cent Store
146. Brenner-Simmons Motel
147. 1st Street Station

148. Fiess-Yunker Mfg. Co.
149. C. Wayne Flynn and Sons
150. Brook Side Jewelers

B. Prepare cross-reference cards for the following names; then place them in the proper alphabetic sequence among cards 101–150. Card 139x, for example, will be among the E's and Card 144x will be among the C's.

1. Christlieb Bakeries, Card 104; cross-reference under Mary Christlieb, Card 104x.
2. Behnke-Walker Business College, Card 112; cross-reference under Walter Behnke, Card 112x.
3. Brazil Exporters, Card 139; cross-reference under Export Committee, Card 139x.
4. Sarah K. Currier, Card 143; cross-reference under Mrs. John Currier, Card 143x.
5. Bergs, Card 144; cross-reference under Conroy's, Inc., Card 144x.
6. Brenner-Simmons Motel, Card 146; cross-reference under Homer Brenner, Card 146x.

C. Prepare an answer sheet.

Exercise 11

See how rapidly you can find the following cards from among those you alphabetized for Exercise 10. As you locate each card, write on an answer sheet the information indicated on the following partially completed answer sheet.

Card No.	Name	Filed After Card No.	Filed Before Card No.
101	*Richard Barbour, Sr.*	*109*	*121*

1. B. Jerry Boorkman
2. State of Florida, Dept. of Labor
3. Doctor Culbertson
4. Fredrickson Kindergarten
5. Bergs
6. Berg of Charleston
7. East-West Bus Co., Inc.
8. Erickson's Market, 225 Everett Street, Portland, Maine 00406
9. Captain John H. Farmer
10. State of Arkansas, Bureau of Mines
11. Richard Barbour, Sr.
12. CGD Corporation
13. Helen Caplan Salon
14. Eckhout-Wilmont Corp.
15. The Boorkman Bros. Hatchery
16. 1st Street Station

Exercise 12

A. Place the following names (151–200) on cards in the proper indexing order; then arrange them in the correct alphabetic sequence.

151. State of California, Dept. of Police
152. Committee for Education, Inc.
153. Dreeson Drugs, Elmira, Illinois 62932
154. Five-Corner Garden Store
155. B and J Automotive Repair
156. David De Luca
157. Federal Savings Bank Denver, Colorado 80215
158. Denver Investment Co.
159. Da Silva Rain Wear Sales Co.
160. Deer Valley Delivery Co.
161. Freeman's
162. The Sam Fuller Agency
163. Da Silva Rainwear Mfg. Co.
164. Mary S. Doan Memorial
165. The Jas. Freeman Grocery
166. Canadian Fisheries, Ltd.
167. Brother Adrian Cigars
168. State of Colorado, Bureau of Fisheries
169. De Land Improvements Corp.
170. Mrs. Diane Burton
171. Carter-Reeves Glass Co.
172. Canadian Fisheries, Inc.
173. Dominion of Canada, Dept. of Health
174. Donald Ehlers & Son
175. Del Bonita Gardeners
176. First Nat. Bank, Deerton, Montana 59025
177. Councilman James Ehler
178. De Kalb Junction
179. Dorothy Carter-Reeves
180. Dreeson Drugs, Campus, Illinois 60920
181. Day's Market, Seymour, Illinois 61875
182. Adams' Bakery, Inc.
183. J. Coddington, Sr.
184. Dr. Amos Cleves
185. Forest Products Industries
186. Delburne Real Estate
187. I. Freeman
188. Adam the Cobbler
189. DTS Supply Co.
190. Frack-Goodwin Car Sales
191. Mrs. Samuel M. De Kalb (Jane L.)
192. James Coddington, Jr.
193. John Henry Forrester
194. Citizens Bank, Adamson, Louisiana 71301
195. Cleve's Bowling Alleys
196. Buford Paint Contractors
197. Day's Market, Seymour, Pennsylvania 17359
198. 40 Staters
199. The Bones-Heath Co.
200. Ehler-James Air Shippers

B. Prepare cross-reference cards for the following names; then place them in the proper alphabetic sequence among Cards 151–200.

1. Committee for Education, Inc., Card 152; cross-reference under Education, Committee (for), Inc., Card 152x.
2. Denver Investment Co., Card 158; cross-reference under Homer R. Carver, Pres., Card 158x.
3. The Sam Fuller Agency, Card 162; cross-reference under Contractors, Paint, Card 162x.
4. Forest Products Industries, Card 185; cross-reference under Chip-Wood, Inc., Card 185x.

5. Delburne Real Estate, Card 186; cross-reference under D. L. Atkinson, Card 186x.
6. James Coddington, Jr., Card 192; cross-reference under Coddington Service, Card 192x.

C. Prepare an answer sheet if one is requested by your instructor.

Exercise 13
Again see how rapidly you can find certain cards—this time from among those you alphabetized for Exercise 12. Prepare an answer sheet as you did for Exercise 11.

1. Mrs. Samuel M. De Kalb (Jane L.)
2. Adam the Cobbler
3. Mary S. Doan Memorial
4. Dominion of Canada, Dept. of Health
5. Citizens Bank, Adamson, Louisiana 71301
6. Donald Ehlers & Son
7. Dr. Amos Cleves
8. The Bones-Heath Co.
9. Da Silva Rain Wear Sales Co.
10. Denver Investment Co.
11. Deer Valley Delivery Co.
12. DTS Supply Co.
13. John Henry Forrester
14. Adams' Bakery, Inc.
15. I. Freeman
16. Frack-Goodwin Car Sales

Exercise 14
Need additional practice in alphabetizing?
A. Arrange Cards 1–50 in correct alphabetic sequence.
B. Prepare an answer sheet if one is requested by your instructor.

Exercise 15
A. From among Cards 1–50 that you alphabetized in Exercise 14, see how quickly you can remove or stand on end the cards for the following ten names. (You may be timed.)

1. Barker
2. Geoffrey M. Du Bois
3. Fargo and Govertsen Corp.
4. Jerry Burns Cab Company
5. Andy the Barber
6. Robert Barnhardt
7. The De Vleming Cooperative
8. Fair Way Nursing Home
9. Albert Cooper
10. Harriet Buford-Field

B. If requested to do so, prepare an answer sheet for this exercise as you did for Exercises 11 and 13.

Exercise 16
More alphabetizing practice:
A. Arrange Cards 51–100 in correct alphabetic sequence.
B. Prepare an answer sheet if one is requested by your instructor.

Exercise 17

More finding practice:

A. From among Cards 51–100 that you alphabetized for Exercise 16, see how quickly you can find the following ten names.

1. De Coursey Radio Merchants
2. Homer A. Becker-Manning
3. The Henri R. D'Abbe Mart
4. ACM Motels
5. Fiess' Cooperative
6. The 4 Sailors' Oyster Bar
7. Commander Estes
8. The Cowan-Fulton Clothing Co.
9. Commerce Dept., Washington, D.C.
10. 4th Avenue Cleaners

B. If requested to do so, prepare an answer sheet for this exercise as you did for Exercises 11 and 13.

Glossary

Abbreviation A shortened form of a word. In indexing, an abbreviation is considered as though it were spelled out.

Accuracy ratio Percent of requested records found during a filing period.

Acronym A word that has been constructed from initials or parts of other words, such as VISTA (Volunteers *in* Service *to* America).

Active file A filing cabinet reserved for records that are used frequently.

Activity ratio Percent of filed records requested during a filing period.

Alphabetic arrangement The listing of names or topics in sequence according to the alphabet. The process is called alphabetizing.

Alphabetic filing Any system in which the captions are names of people, organizations, or letters of the alphabet.

Alphabetize To arrange in sequence according to the letters of the alphabet.

Archives The historical records kept by an organization.

Auxiliary guide See *Secondary guide.*

Backshifting Shifting the location of records to allow for expansion at the beginning of a file.

Cabinet A container with one or more drawers for housing filed records.

Caption A name, letter, or number under which records are filed.

Card filing Processing and storing business information on cards. There are two kinds of card files—vertical and visible.

Carrier folder A folder, usually of a distinctive color and made of a strong material, that is used to transport records.

Centralized control A plan of organization whereby one person is responsible for all records management in the organization, whether files are centralized or decentralized.

Centralized files Files in which all records except highly specialized departmental ones are stored together.

Charge method A procedure used to account for records that have been removed from the files.

Chronological In sequence according to date. When records are filed chronologically, the record bearing the latest date is usually in front.

Classifying Arranging in groups according to a predetermined plan.

Coding The process of marking correspondence with the caption under which it will be stored.

Commercial system A set of ready-made guides and folders manufactured for immediate use.

Compound geographic name The name of a city, state, or other geographical location that includes more than one word.

Consultant   One who gives professional advice, in this case concerning the operation and maintenance of files and records.

Correspondence   Any written communication that has not been designed to be placed in a card or forms file.

Cross-filing   See *Cross-reference.*

Cross-reference   A notation in a file or an index showing that the record being sought is stored elsewhere; or the filing of a duplicate of an original record in other locations where it might be sought.

Cut   The size of the tab on the back flap of a folder, usually expressed in a fraction. *One-half cut,* for example, means that the tab takes up one-half of the back flap of a folder.

Cycle method   See *Two-period transfer.*

Data filing   See *Subject filing.*

Date-stamp   A notation on an incoming piece of correspondence to indicate the date and, often, the hour of receipt.

Decentralized files   See *Departmental files.*

Decentralized files with centralized control   Departmental files kept according to regulations of a central authority in the organization.

Decimal numeric   A subject system widely used in libraries in which headings, divisions, subdivisions, etc., are identified by numbers such as 300., 310., 311., and 311.1.

Degree   An educational award, such as Doctor of Education (Ed.D.), that is conferred for certain advanced studies. Degree titles, such as Doctor, are not filing units when they precede the full name of an individual.

Departmental files   Files in which records of one department are stored separately from records of other departments.

Desk trays   Containers for incoming and outgoing correspondence kept on desks.

Dictionary arrangement   Organization of a subject file with headings that do not have divisions or subdivisions.

Direct   A filing system that permits the location of records without reference to an index.

Disposing, disposition   Destroying or eliminating records that are no longer needed.

Double capacity   See *Two-period transfer.*

Duplex numeric   A subject system in which headings, divisions, subdivisions, etc., are identified by a number, a dash, a second number, a dash, a third number, etc. Some duplex-numeric systems use a combination of numbers and letters and some use only numbers (e. g., 3, 3-1, 3-1-1, 3-1-1-1).

Electric   Refers to the operation of automatic files and data processing machines by means of an electric motor.

Electronic   Refers to machines that process data by means of electric current and a minimum of moving parts.

Encyclopedic arrangement   Organization of a subject file with main headings, divisions, and subdivisions.

Equipment   The cabinets, furniture, and miscellaneous devices used in handling and storing records.

Expansion   Any increase in the amount of equipment and supplies to make possible the storing of more records.

File cards   Cardboard slips that are used in both vertical and visible files.

File shelf   A shelf that is attached to the front or the side of a file drawer to hold records during filing and finding operations.

File worker   An employee whose specialized job is to inspect, index, code, sort, and store records and to remove them from the files when they are needed.

Files Containers for storing records—cabinets, open shelves, boxes, or any other type of housing.

Filing The process of classifying, arranging, and storing records so that they can be obtained quickly when needed.

Filing period The span of time during which records remain in the active files.

Filing system An arrangement of equipment and supplies to permit the storing of records according to a definite plan.

Film-reading machine See *Reader*.

Flowchart The diagram of an operation on paper, from its beginning to its end, so that all of its steps can be easily seen and evaluated.

Folder A manila or fiber container that holds correspondence in files.

Follow-up A system of checking on borrowed records to effect their return to the files.

Follow-up file A file that calls attention to either (1) charged-out records or (2) an office job that requires action on a certain date. It is usually arranged chronologically.

Follow-up folder A folder with dates along the top edge that can be clearly marked with a signal indicating when the records within the folder require action.

Followers or compressors Movable supports that expand or contract the usable space within a file drawer.

Forms analysis A study of whether a form is needed and what static information it should contain, in what sequence and design.

Forms file A file used for the storage of either blank or filled-out forms.

Geographic filing An alphabetic arrangement of records by location.

Given name An individual's first name.

Guide A sheet of heavy cardboard with a tab and caption, which is used to guide the eye to the desired section in a file drawer. A guide also serves as a support for the records in the drawer.

Hyphenated name An individual or organization name that consists of words or letters connected by a hyphen. A hyphenated surname is considered as *one* unit for indexing whereas hyphenated words in a firm name are considered as separate units.

Inactive Records not subject to frequent use, which are stored in less accessible and less costly equipment than active records.

Index card record A card, such as an address file card, that is used primarily as a reference to other information.

Indexing Selecting the caption under which a record is to be filed.

Indexing arrangement The order in which the units of a name are considered for filing.

Indirect A filing system that usually requires reference to an index before records can be found.

Individual folder A folder that contains records concerning only one correspondent or subject.

Information maintenance Keeping data in a form that makes it usable.

Information processing Changing the form of data to make it usable.

Information retrieval Getting information out of a manual or electronic storage device.

Input The information put into a business system.

Inspecting Checking the correspondence for a release mark before indexing.

Kraft   Heavyweight paper used for file guides and folders.

Label   A sticker that is attached to the tab of a guide or a folder and on which the caption appears.

Lateral file   A file cabinet in which records are stored perpendicular to the opening to the file.

Legal name   (1) A man's full name. (2) A single woman's full name.   (3) A married woman's first and middle or first and maiden names combined with her husband's surname.

Manila   Medium weight pressboard used for file folders.

Maximum-minimum transfer   A plan for periodically transferring records from active to transfer files.   A maximum and a minimum period of time are set for storing records in the active files.

Microfiche   Miniature filmed records in card form.

Microfilming   Photographing records and reducing them greatly so they can be stored on filmstrips, cards, or rolls.

Middle-digit filing   A numeric arrangement of records according to the middle, rather than the first, digits.

Miscellaneous folder   A folder that contains records for correspondents or subjects not active enough to warrant individual folders.

Misfile   To store a record in the wrong location.

Multiple transfer   See *Two-period transfer.*

Name file   A card file containing identifying information about names.

Numeric filing   The filing of correspondence or cards according to numbers.

One-period transfer   A plan in which the active files contain records for the current filing period only.   At predetermined intervals all the records are transferred.

Open-shelf filing   A method of filing in which shelves, rather than filing cabinets with drawers, are used to house records.

Out folder   A folder used to store correspondence while the regular folder is out of the files.   It indicates that the regular folder has been borrowed and gives the name of the borrower.

Out guide   A guide used to indicate that an entire folder has been removed from the files.

Periodic transfer   The removal of records at predetermined intervals from the current active files to the inactive or transfer files.

Perpetual transfer   The transfer of records from the current to the inactive files on the basis of activity rather than predetermined filing periods.

Political division   An area created by law, such as a town, city, county, state, or nation.

Position   The location, counting from left to right, of the tab on a guide or folder.

Possessive   A word indicating ownership that usually contains an apostrophe.   In indexing, only the letters up to the apostrophe are considered.

Posted card record   A card on which information is recorded frequently as part of the day-to-day operations of the organization.

Preposition   A word used to connect a noun or a pronoun with some other word.   Prepositions, such as *for, in,* and *of,* are disregarded in indexing.

Primary guide   The main guide for a section of filed records.

Punched card   A $7\frac{3}{8}$- by $3\frac{1}{4}$-inch card record that is coded with small punched holes and processed on data processing machines.

Reader   A machine used to view microfilms.

Recharge form   A slip used to charge out records when they are passed from one person to another without being returned to the files.

Records   All information that is kept by an organization, whether it is in the form of correspondence, cards, tapes, or microfilm.

Records management   Planning, organizing, and controlling the creation, protection, use, storage, and disposition of records.

Reference   The directing of an individual's attention to a source of information.

Register   A list of correspondents and the numbers assigned to them in a numeric correspondence file.

Relative index   An alphabetic list of all the headings and subheadings in a subject file.

Release mark   A notation showing that a record has received the required attention and is ready for filing.

Requisition slip   A form used to request records from the files.

Retention period   The length of time records are kept before being discarded.

Routing form   A slip attached to charged-out records indicating the sequence in which they are to be delivered to several individuals in an organization before being returned to the files.

Scores   Creases along the front flap of a folder that allow for expansion.

Secondary guide   A guide that subdivides the section of a file controlled by a primary guide.

Security center   Underground or isolated storage place for very valuable records.

Selective copying   A feature of multiple-copy specialty forms that prevents some of the information recorded on the first sheet from being copied on other sheets.

Self-mailer   A form designed so that it can be mailed back to the sender without being placed in an envelope.

Signals   Plastic, metal, or paper devices that are used to guide the eye to pertinent information, usually in card and visible files.

Sorting   Arranging records in sequence after they have been coded to facilitate storing.

Special guide   See *Secondary guide.*

Staggered arrangement   Placement of guide or folder tabs in successive positions from left to right.

Static information   All of the printed information on a form before it is filled in.

Storing   The placing of records in a file container.

Subject filing   The alphabetic arrangement of records by names of topics or things.

Substitution card   A card used to replace records removed from a file folder. This card indicates the name of the borrower.

Supervisor   The person who is responsible for the operation and maintenance of files and filing systems.

Surname   The last name of an individual.

Surname prefix   That part of a surname that precedes the body of the surname, such as *De, Fitz, Mac, O',* and *Von.* These prefixes are indexed as part of the surname.

Systems and procedures A system is a series of related steps followed in accomplishing a major office activity. A procedure is a series of related substeps performed to carry out part of a system. For example, the procedure for figuring hours worked from a timecard is part of the larger payroll system.

Tab The projection above the body of a guide or folder on which the caption appears.

Template A scale-size cutout or stencil of equipment that is used in planning layout.

Terminal-digit filing A numeric arrangement of records according to the last, rather than the first, digits.

Tickler file See *Follow-up file.*

Title A word indicating rank, office, or privilege. A title is considered an indexing unit only when it precedes a single name.

Topical filing See *Subject filing.*

Transfer Removal of records from the active files to inactive files.

Transfer file or box A container that houses transferred records. This container is usually constructed of inexpensive cardboard or metal materials.

Transpose To rearrange the normal order of a name; for example, *Donald Windham* transposed is *Windham, Donald.*

Two-period transfer A plan in which the active files provide space for current records and records from the last filing period. At transfer time, only the oldest records are removed.

Unit Each part of a name used in indexing.

Variable information Data filled in on a form.

Vertical filing The storage of records on edge.

Visible filing Storage of cards in specially designed equipment so that the information near the edges of the cards can be seen easily.

Work station Location of one employee's equipment and materials in an office (desk, chair, file, etc.).

Bibliography

Following is a list of books and periodicals that contain information about the management and use of business records systems. These works were selected for: (1) instructors who wish to provide college-level supplementary reading and introduce advanced filing and records management applications in their courses and (2) office managers and others seeking detailed or technical insight for the solution of specific records management problems. In addition to those listed, nearly every book and periodical on office or secretarial practice includes some information about filing. A list of such publications would be very long and is therefore not given.

Books

Benedon, William, *Records Management*, Prentice-Hall, Inc., Englewood Cliffs, N.J., 1969.

Bourne, Charles P., *Methods of Information Handling*, John Wiley & Sons, Inc., New York, 1963.

Checklist for Appraising Files Operation in Your Office, General Services Administration, National Archives and Records Service, Washington, D.C., 1968.

Elliott, C. Orville, and Robert S. Wasley, *Business Information Processing Systems*, Richard D. Irwin, Inc., Homewood, Ill., 1965.

Griffin, Mary Claire, *Records Management, A Modern Tool for Business*, Allyn and Bacon, Inc., Boston, 1964.

Guide to Record Retention Requirements, Government Printing Office, Washington, D.C., 1966.

Johnson, Mina M., and Norman F. Kallaus, *Records Management*, South-Western Publishing Company, Cincinnati, 1967.

Leahy, Emmett J., and Christopher A. Cameron, *Modern Records Management*, McGraw-Hill Book Company, New York, 1965.

Neuner, John J. W., and B. Lewis Keeling, *Administrative Office Management*, South-Western Publishing Company, Cincinnati, 1966.

Place, Irene, and Estelle L. Popham, *Filing and Records Management,* Prentice-Hall, Inc., Englewood Cliffs, N.J., 1966.

Prince, Thomas R., *Information Systems for Management Planning and Control,* Richard D. Irwin, Inc., Homewood, Ill., 1966.

Terry, George R., *Office Management and Control,* Richard D. Irwin, Inc., Homewood, Ill., 1970.

Weeks, Bertha M., *Filing and Records Management,* The Ronald Press Company, New York, 1964.

Periodicals

Administrative Management, 212 Fifth Avenue, New York, N.Y. 10010.

Advanced Management Journal, 16 West 40th Street, New York, N.Y. 10018.

American Archivist, Wayne State University, Detroit, Mich. 48202.

The AMS Management Bulletins, Maryland Avenue, Willow Grove, Pa. 19090.

Business Automation, 288 Park Avenue, West, Elmhurst, Ill. 60126.

Computers and Automation, 815 Washington Street, Newtonville, Mass. 02160.

Data Processing Digest, 1140 South Robertson Boulevard, Los Angeles, Calif. 90035.

Data Processing for Education, 410 Book Building, Detroit, Mich. 48226.

Data Processing Magazine, 134 North 13th Street, Philadelphia, Pa. 19107.

Data Processor, International Business Machines Corporation, 112 East Post Road, White Plains, N.Y. 10601.

Datamation, 35 Mason Street, Greenwich, Conn. 06830.

Digital Computer Newsletter, Information Systems Branch, Office of Naval Research, Washington, D.C. 20360.

Journal of Data Education, Norwich University, Northfield, Vt. 05663.

Journal of Data Management, 505 Busse Highway, Park Ridge, Ill. 60068.

Management Review, 135 West 50th Street, New York, N.Y. 10020.

Modern Office Procedures, 614 Superior Avenue, West, Cleveland, Ohio 44113.

The Office, 73 Southfield Avenue, Stamford, Conn. 06904.

Systems and Procedures, 24587 Bagley Road, Cleveland, Ohio 44138.

Today's Secretary, 330 West 42nd Street, New York, N.Y. 10036.

Index